THE PEMBROKESHIRE
COASTAL PATH

Elegug Stacks from Flimston Head

THE PEMBROKESHIRE COASTAL PATH

A Walk for All Seasons

by

Dennis R. Kelsall

CICERONE PRESS
MILNTHORPE, CUMBRIA, UK

ISBN 1 85284 186 9
A catalogue record for this book is available from the British Library.

ACKNOWLEDGEMENTS

My thanks go to a number of people who have supported me with help and information during the writing of this guide. First to Jan, my wife, whose entire lifestyle has been disrupted, either as a result of hectic weekends re-walking the path or long evenings spent deciphering my notes. She has been uncomplaining throughout and has helped immensely in collating information and keeping me organised. In searching for an initial field base near Amroth, we found John and Madeline. Their sense of humour and generous hospitality led us to return there on our successive visits, and assuaged the effects that regular Friday night journeys from Lancashire created. Their kindness will always be appreciated.

David Matthews and the staff of the Pembrokeshire Coast National Park Authority provided me with much useful information, and I am grateful for permission to use material produced in the various National Park Information Guides. I am also grateful to Lieutenant-Colonel Portman of Castlemartin RAC Range for his time spent in briefing me on the history of the ranges. A number of other people also responded to my requests for help and information: Sue Denny of the RNLI, Sue Ward of the RSPB on Ramsey, Mr H. Cooper at Trinity House, Mr and Mrs Scourfield Lewis of Colby, and Mr A. Warlow of Gulf Oil for which I thank them. Thanks also go to the many people I met along the coast whose comment and observation was both interesting and useful, and to the two people who offered me, a total stranger, free bed and board for the night; such acts of generosity restore my faith in human kindness.

Finally, but not least, I must thank Terry whose idea this book was. Without his encouragement and positive criticism, it would never have been written.

Front Cover: Westdale Bay

CONTENTS

ADVICE TO READERS

Readers are advised that whilst every effort is taken by the author to ensure the accuracy of this guidebook, changes can occur which may affect the contents. A book of this nature with detailed descriptions and detailed maps is more prone to change than a more general guide. New fences and stiles appear, waymarking alters, there may be new buildings or eradication of old buildings. It is advisable to check locally on transport, accommodation, shops etc. but even rights of way can be altered, paths can be eradicated by landslip, forest clearances or changes of ownership. The publisher would welcome notes of any such changes.

INTRODUCTION

THE PEMBROKESHIRE COASTAL PATH

The Welsh Pen-Fro means Land's End and aptly describes this south-western corner of Wales; a long and much indented peninsula bounded by sea on three sides, its western extremities facing the Atlantic ocean. Pembrokeshire, now part of the county of Dyfed, has some of the finest coastal scenery in the country. Its great natural beauty and diversity were factors that led to the creation of a National Park in 1952, to protect the coast and the wildlife that abounds on it. Virtually the whole of the county's coastline, together with a wide sweep of land behind was designated, only the industrial and urban conurbations of Pembroke Dock, Milford Haven and Fishguard being excluded. The wild beauty of the Mynydd Preseli that dominate the north-eastern corner of the old county and the secretive tidal reaches of the Daugleddau twisting their way deep into the heart of the countryside from its south-western tip were also included. For its overall area, it has possibly the greatest natural diversity of any of Britain's National Parks.

The year following the Park's designation, approval was given to create a continuous footpath around the coast, and work commenced to establish what has become one of Britain's most splendid long distance footpaths. Although the coast had for millennia provided the most effective communication and transport route between the numerous settlements scattered around its shores, travel had been by boat rather than land. Therefore no traditional course existed that could be followed. Indeed in many places there was not even a public right of access to the coast. The creation of the Coast Path took a considerable amount of time. Much negotiation and discussion was needed to establish rights of way with the many, and not always sympathetic landowners along its length. That was, perhaps, as monumental a task as the subsequent construction necessary to take the Path across often difficult and much overgrown cliff tops.

In 1970, the Coast Path was officially opened, linking the village of Amroth on the south-eastern boundary of the county to St Dogmael's at its north-eastern corner. Although for much of its way the route follows either the cliff edge or high water mark, there are occasional necessary deviations inland, mainly to avoid military or industrial complexes. The Path passes the industrialisation of Pembroke Dock and Milford Haven and the holiday towns of Saundersfoot and Tenby. However, these diversions and encounters are brief, and for most of its way the Coast Path exhilarates in the unspoilt beauty that divides two vastly different and often opposing aspects of nature: the land and sea. Often the route lies along the untouched fringes of cultivation that have previously had little or no practical value and where nature has been allowed to evolve with little interference from man. Sometimes wild and remote, elsewhere just forgotten corners that have been missed in man's eagerness for development, these places have become havens for plants, birds and animals often increasingly marginalised by modern practices.

However, nothing remains static and unceasing efforts on the part of National Park staff are necessary to conserve a clear passage along the Path's length. Winter storms, the natural regeneration of vegetation and the tramp of countless feet collectively create a maintenance task of "Forth Bridge" magnitude, except that this has a length of some 290 kilometres (180 miles). Improvements in access to the coastal strip have also been achieved since the Path's conception. Re-assessment of need and a more co-operative approach to operational management by the Army has enabled the opening of some previously prohibited sections of coast for public use. It was not until the late 1960s that public access between Broad Haven and St Govan's was generally possible; the section between Lydstep and Skrinkle Haven was not opened until 1983. More recently, although general public access remains prohibited, guided walks organised by National Park staff allow an opportunity to appreciate the spectacular limestone cliffs around Linney Head. Industrial presence also changes; two of the large oil installations that once overlooked Milford Haven have now been largely dismantled, the remaining contoured platforms on which the massive storage tanks previously rested are cloaked in green and present much less of a visual intrusion than before.

Indeed, it is a point to remember that many of the "natural wildernesses" encountered around the coast are, in fact, the abandoned industrial and military sites of earlier centuries. Similarly, most of the now quiet harbours and tiny villages that punctuate the cliffs were not that long ago busily engaged in trade. Pembrokeshire satisfied

PEMBROKESHIRE COASTAL PATH

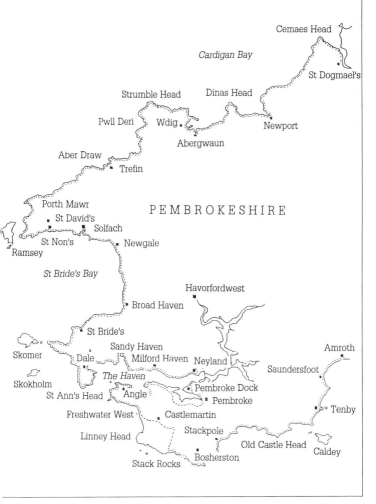

Cemaes Head

Cardigan Bay

St Dogmael's

Strumble Head   Dinas Head

Pwll Deri   Wdig.   Newport

Abergwaun

Aber Draw

Trefin

PEMBROKESHIRE

Porth Mawr

St David's

Solfach

St Non's   Newgale

Ramsey

St Bride's Bay

Havorfordwest

Broad Haven

St Bride's

Sandy Haven   Amroth

Skomer   Dale   Milford Haven   Neyland

Saundersfoot

The Haven

Skokholm   Pembroke Dock

St Ann's Head   Angle   Pembroke

Tenby

Freshwater West   Castlemartin

Stackpole

Linney Head   Old Castle Head   Caldey

Bosherston

Stack Rocks

many markets at home and abroad with the products of its rich farmland, fishing fleets, mines and quarries, and their exploitation brought prosperity for many. Our nostalgic vision of the enterprise of earlier ages might help retain a perspective on today's industrial and commercial activity. Industry is important to the local economy, and development will undoubtedly continue. However, the controls exercised by virtue of its status as a National Park, a greater awareness of environmental needs and the pressures of the people who both live in and visit the region should maintain a balanced approach for the future.

The necessity to pass through pockets of industrialisation should not be a deterrent to walking the Path in its entirety. The encounter with pavements and urbanisation is brief; the route invariably manages to find hidden undeveloped corners, or discover something of interest to distract the attention. Although the far view may sometimes be imperfected by a factory chimney or housing estate or the sea-front be encased in concrete, the walker is usually able to observe from a distance, and remain uninvolved. Even in towns and beside industrial complexes there is something of interest for those prepared to look; the relics of bygone ages line the path and there is a level at which both nature and man can co-exist. In any case those few kilometres are more than amply compensated by the vast sections of inviolate wildness.

The Pembrokeshire Coastal Path provides an almost unique association of natural beauty, habitat, variety and mood, which is readily accessible to lovers of the countryside throughout the year. The country's complex geology and the effects of erosion have combined to create a coastal strip of outstanding scenic attraction. The coast line's favourable association with the relatively warm waters of the Gulf Stream has created a multiplicity of rich and varied habitats promoting an immense range of plant and animal life. Relative inaccessibility and the impracticality of the use of this narrow ribbon of land has allowed many plants, animals and birds to retain a foothold, and the re-introduction of traditional land management techniques in some areas is actually encouraging the re-establishment of species.

AN OUTLINE OF THE GEOLOGY OF THE REGION

A spectrum of the region's geology is portrayed by the record contained in the successive layers of rock that are revealed along its perimeter. Successive periods of volcanic activity, sedimentation and accumulation have been distorted by massive earth movements and erosion to create the complex structure of the Pembroke peninsula. An almost unbroken geological sequence can be traced in its rocks, the earliest being dated at over 3,000 million years (Ma) old and the latest, coal, formed a mere 280 Ma ago.

The oldest rocks are hard igneous and volcanic pre-Cambrian granites, which underlie the whole of the region, outcropping on Ramsey and at the southern tip of the St David's peninsula. Later sedimentation in the Cambrian era, between 500 and 570 Ma ago, produced sandstones, which are now exposed along the northern coast of St Bride's Bay and whose fine properties were exploited in the building of the cathedral at St David's. The next 65 million years are classed as the Ordovician geological period, in which fine muds laid down at the bottom of an ancient sea were compressed to produce shales, rich in the fossils of early marine life. Periods of intense volcanic activity during that era added further complexity with both intrusions and surface flows to create tracts of harder rock. These Ordovician rocks dominate the northern Pembrokeshire coast, the footpath from St David's Head to Fishguard being alternately striped by softer multi-layered slates, shales and volcanic rocks. The relative resistance to erosion of these products of subterranean activity has left a line of isolated hills along the coast from Carn Llidi to Garn Fawr and determined the headlands of St David's and Strumble. Volcanic outcrops also form the basis of the Mynydd Preseli. A succession of limestone, shale and conglomerate associated with the ensuing Silurian period, some 435 to 395 Ma ago, can be seen along the southern Marloes peninsula, overlying a contemporary volcanic feature that is exposed on the northern side of the peninsula and continues beyond Skomer to the offshore islands beyond.

The end of the long period of sedimentation is defined by the collision of a continental mass composed of north-western Scotland, Greenland and Labrador with that of Europe. This event, known as the Caledonian orogeny, created many of Britain's present mountain regions and produced a SW-NE folding across northern

Pembrokeshire which raised the St David's peninsula. A combination of rapid erosion of the newly created mountain areas and the hot dry conditions existing in the area during the Devonian period (395-345 Ma ago) led to the formation of the Red Sandstones that now dominate the coasts of the Haven and the southern shore of St Bride's Bay. During the later Carboniferous era (345-280 Ma ago), climatic and land level changes created a warm sea in which the limestones, exposed between St Govan's and Castlemartin, and subsequent deposits of millstone grit, appearing to the north of Tenby, were formed. The youngest rocks visible along the coast are coal measures, created as the Carboniferous period came to an end; sea levels fell, leaving a vast region of tropical swamp that was lavishly exploited by plant life. The exclusion of oxygen retarded decomposition in the steady accretion of plant debris, and subsequent compression of this organic mass by the weight of later sedimentation produced coal, which now outcrops along the eastern shore of St Bride's Bay and between Amroth and Saundersfoot.

A further period of earth movement, originating in what is now north-western France, pushed from the south-west to fold these new layers of rocks and complicate the earlier period of plication to again produce hills and ridges. However, these hills, together with the sediments and accretions of the last 280 Ma, have been largely removed with the erosion caused by rising sea levels some 17 Ma ago. This planing action of the sea has removed the overlying softer rocks, resulting in the plateau at about 60 metres (200 feet) above present sea level, which predominates much of the county. Areas of harder rock, largely those of more ancient volcanic origin, survived as islands until sea levels fell once again, leaving them as hills above the plateau.

The contours produced by earth movements and changing sea levels have been subsequently modified by ice and water. Today's drainage pattern was superimposed upon the landscape at the end of the last Ice Age, some 20,000 years ago. Southern Wales was at the southern limit of a gigantic glacier that originated in the west of Scotland and flowed south, completely filling the Irish Sea basin. Moving ice scoured channels, the debris being carried south and later deposited as it began to melt. It was this process that left deposits of sand and gravel, such as those seen at Dale and to the south of Tenby. As a warmer climate developed, vast quantities of meltwater flowed in torrents to the sea, then some 90 metres (300 feet) lower than its present level, with sufficient power to gouge deep drainage patterns into the rock. Today the magnitude of these valleys, which create abrupt clefts in the cliffs, is out of all proportion to the modest streams now flowing through them to the sea. Such a monumental release of water caused sea levels to rise to present levels and the lower reaches of the valleys were flooded. Erosion patterns have left a number of these drowned valleys or rias around the coast, and their attributes of shelter and deep water access have been exploited as harbours; those at Solfach and Milford Haven are fine examples.

The process of change will never finish; the sea steadily gnaws at the base of today's cliffs and is creating another plateau that can be seen at low water in impressive areas of wave cut platform. Wind blown sand is accumulating to create dune systems, and the weather is persistently softening the contours of the land. The debris is washed away to contribute to the accretion of sediment below the sea and thus form the substance of some future land.

A BRIEF HISTORY OF THE AREA

Early stone-based cultures have left little evidence of their existence in the region. Discoveries of fragments of domestic refuse in caves on Caldey suggest that pre-glacial Old Stone Age tribes passed through the area some 50,000 years ago, but as the climate cooled with the advancing ice sheets, they returned to the south. Later warmer conditions saw a migration of Mesolithic cultures in about 8,000 BC. Again they left few traces, but some sites such as the "flint factories" that have been identified at, for example Little Furznip, point to their activity. Flint is not native here and is thought to have been carried from Ireland in the glacial ice and released around the shores as it melted. More substantial visible evidence of early man relates to a later period at around 3,000 BC, when Neolithic farmers established themselves around the coast. Their settlement can be identified from traces of hut circles and burial sites and there are a number of impressive dolmens to be seen along the Path.

By the time of the Bronze Age, the peninsula had become a highway, connecting settlements in the south with a sea passage to Ireland. Burial mounds and standing stones line the ancient routes, and it is believed that the Bluestones for Stonehenge were transported along these routes from the Mynydd Preseli. From 300 BC, successive Iron Age tribes settled around the coast, originating probably in Brittany. They were responsible for the innumerable promontory forts encountered along the length of the Path, and on St David's Head their old field patterns, dating back some 2,000 years, can still be discerned on the sloping hillsides. The Roman invasion of Britain apparently had little influence on the way of life in this far corner of the land, and fishing, farming and trade perhaps remained the major preoccupations of its people.

By 400 AD a considerable change was taking place and heralded the "Great Age of Saints". Christianity, and the knowledge and learning that accompanied it, established itself around the shores of the Irish Sea. St David's is just one of many settlements that were founded by those early Christians, and their organisation and constant travel encouraged stability and trade in the area. Many of the ancient landings and chapels around the coast betray their association with those saints in their names. These beneficial influences continued for some 400 years until adventurous Vikings discovered the rich pickings that were to be had around the shores of the country. More interested in plunder than settlement, they destroyed many of the Celtic communities that had been built up and disrupted the civilisation that was starting to develop. Their passing is remembered in the Nordic names that survive around the coast.

1066 saw the arrival of the Normans in England. Their movement across the country was rapid, and within 30 years they had established themselves in the fertile southern corner of Pembrokeshire. They largely ignored the less productive and inhospitable lands to the north and there, traditional indigenous cultures continued. The effects of that separation can still be seen on today's maps: Welsh names predominate northern Pembrokeshire whilst "English" names are more common in the south. Although invaders, they settled with the Welsh and laid the foundations of a prosperity based on agriculture, coastal and continental trade, and fishing that was to continue through to the industrial revolution and beyond. Subsequent threats of invasion, the passage of kings and civil war have all caused Pembrokeshire to be mentioned in history books, but have done little to change its destiny.

The early industrialisation of Britain brought with it an increasing demand for food, fuel and raw materials such as iron and stone. Every landing in Pembrokeshire was exploited and the coast became ringed with busy harbours, exporting goods to industrial centres in an armada of trading ships. The growing revolution later saw the development of a new form of transport, the railway. Although eventually its tracks arrived at Tenby, Neyland and Fishguard, the region had by then become isolated and within a short space of time its busy coastal traffic declined in favour of the quicker and more efficient railways that were spreading as arteries throughout the rest of Britain. Yet, initiatives were taken. Nineteenth-century entrepreneurs came to the Cleddau estuary with visions of a prosperity based on a naval dockyard and trade with Ireland and America. Brunel brought his railway, and docks, harbours and fortifications were built; local industry developed to support the growing commerce.

However, the promise was short lived; relative remoteness and the vagaries of trade and politics combined to frustrate economic development and by the beginning of this century Pembroke had lost its commercial position. Even the invention of the automobile and the consequent improvements to the country's road system that it brought did little to revitalise a region that had by then become largely remote from the industrial centres of Britain.

A developing tourist industry and a periodic resurgence of the defensive and military importance of the area brought Pembrokeshire through the first half of this century. However, little major investment took place until the early 1960s, when the oil companies recognised the value of Milford Haven as a deep-water harbour. Development took place at a phenomenal rate, with ultimately five refineries being constructed around its shore. A massive oil burning power station soon followed. This unprecedented industrialisation by both visually and environmentally highly intrusive industries gave rise to serious concern about the future of the whole area, resulting in the formation of the Milford Haven Harbour Conservancy Board, to promote conservation issues and contribute to preserving standards in the environment. A growing awareness and sense of responsibility by industry has now generated some optimism for the environment's future.

The decline in the late 1980s of the demand for oil and its products and the more general country-wide recession has once again affected the economy of the area, with many jobs being lost as a result. New industries are still coming to the area, but are unable to replace the former employment opportunities offered by the large industries. Leisure and tourism are now seen by many as a major contributor in supporting the economic future of the area. The tradition of holiday resorts has long been established. Tenby led the way in the late eighteenth century when it became a fashionable spa, and others followed. The established resorts have managed to maintain their character and yet have adapted to satisfy the changing fashions of the British family holiday. They remain a popular annual destination for many of today's generation. The former nineteenth century industrial centres of the Haven are being given a new lease of life, with marinas and leisure infrastructures being developed to attract recreational sailors. As with everything, a balance needs to be maintained; intensive and intrusive recreational use of an area is as equally capable of damaging the environment as heavy industry. The uniqueness of the Pembrokeshire National Park derives from its diverse past, and its future will depend equally on a harmony of interests.

FLORA AND FAUNA

The rich variety and abundance of wildlife around the coast owes its existence to the combined influences of climate, topography and the hand of man. A hundred years ago the coast was described by the Victorian writer Gosse as a place that "teams with treasures, where the naturalist may see in a day's excursion what in ordinary circumstances would count a fair harvest in a week". That observation thankfully remains valid today with a plethora of distinct and varied habitats offering sites for both land and sea species.

The inaccessible cliffs and offshore islands provide relative safety from predators and attract vast numbers of seabirds who come to establish nests. Many of the major sites are now further protected by their designation as reserves. Skomer, Skokholm, Grassholm, St Margaret's and Ramsey are particularly important, providing breeding grounds for many species. These include gannets, fulmars, manx shearwaters, storm petrels, shags, cormorants, kittiwakes and other species of gull, terns, guillemot, puffin and, of course, the Park's emblem, the razorbill.

Land birds are an equally common sight; crows, jackdaws and ravens scavenge for carrion and small prey along the cliff tops, and chough are establishing themselves at several places along the coast. Predatory birds such as buzzards and kestrels also patrol the cliff margins, and peregrine falcons have established nest sites in a number of places. Less obvious but equally prolific are the many small birds that flit amongst the rocks or perch on the low bushes, such as rock pipits, stonechats and wheatears, adding their songs to the wash of the waves. Although much of the coast is composed of rocky cliffs, there are a number of tidal estuaries that favour ducks and waders, notably the higher reaches of the Nyfer and Haven estuaries and Angle Bay.

The same diversity is to be seen in the plant life that abounds. Habitats range from bleak windswept cliff tops over which gales can drive salt spray far inland, stunting plant growth and giving trees, where they survive, a wind ravished gait. By contrast, tucked behind folds are sheltered valleys, lush with woodland and marshy meadows. Long stretches of the coast are sheltered from the prevailing winds, and there, even on the high cliff tops, full woodland can develop. The abrupt twists and turns and ups and downs of the coast and the markedly different soil types can create vastly different environments within the space of a few yards. Even a sudden turn of the cliff can provide enough shelter for a mass of delicate flowers to sprout out of bare crevices and the shallow depression of a small stream is sufficient to create a separate micro climate. The beach-heads themselves provide further variety, in the dune systems and shingle bars that lie barely out of reach from the waves, often protecting a salt marsh at the foot of the valley behind. The hand of man has contributed to these environments with ancient hedgerows and traditional field embankments, which add their own distinctiveness and charm.

The diversity of species and habitat creates a dazzling array of flowers and plants that even the most un-botanical walker can but fail to appreciate. From the beginning of the year the barest cliffs awaken with a mass of delicate colour and the wind-battered hillsides become cloaked with new life that persists through the autumn. A succession of plants burst into leaf, flower and fruit, before finally contributing to the rich golden hue of the closing year. Violets, primroses and celandines herald the awakening of spring, and as summer approaches, bluebells, campion and thrift colour the woods and cliffs with their blooms. In full summer the cliff banks are a mass of yellow and the air heavy with the almost sickly smell of gorse bushes, and in autumn vast thickets of blackberries provide tasty pickings for both walker and birds. Even in winter, over 40 species of plant have been found to be in flower. The sheer number of species precludes the practicality of a list in a work such as this, but every walker embarking on the path would do well to create space in their pocket for at least a small field guide.

Insects and animal life exploit this rich habitat and complete a complex food chain. In spring and summer the air can be thick with the scent of wild flowers and literally humming with the noise of all manner of flying insects. Adders are not uncommon in some areas and although shy creatures, you may come across one basking on a rock in the sun. Small rodents and rabbits are food for buzzards and other hunters, and even if you do not see a fox trotting through the undergrowth, you will certainly detect their passing from the obnoxious scent they leave as identification of their territorial rights. Less obvious are the secretive badgers, but their sets are plentiful along the coast, and otters play in the waters of Bosherston lily ponds. Atlantic grey seals surround the coast, and in autumn come to the shores of the islands and unreachable coves below the cliffs to give birth and suckle their pups.

WALKING THE PATH

The Pembrokeshire Coastal Path offers some of the finest walking in Britain, with many kilometres of unbroken natural beauty providing an ever-changing experience of unfettered creation. The juxtaposition of land and sea create a special magic that few such long distance trails can provide. Its twisting nature, although often presenting a panorama along many kilometres of cliff, can tantalisingly conceal the next tiny cove or valley. Each turned corner reveals something fresh in the vegetation, rocks or scene. At any time of the year there is much to see, and for bird watchers or plant lovers, the Path is truly a paradise. Short lengths of the way pass through towns and villages but the majority is along open coast where you may hardly meet another person all day.

TOPOGRAPHY

Throughout its length the route generally follows paths, tracks and in places the beach, occasionally resorting to lanes or roads. The terrain varies enormously, some sections being almost level upon good stable ground, while others present a succession of steep climbs that demand strenuous walking, particularly for those carrying a backpack. These parts are definitely not for the unfit. Along many of the steepest sections steps have been constructed, but elsewhere the way may lie over steep grass or rocky banks. Care is needed in wet weather since grass and rock is often slippery and some places can become quite muddy. As long as you remember on which side the sea was when you started off, there are few serious navigation problems and discrete Coast Path signs will keep you on your way. For the experienced walker the completion of the Path presents few problems and for those making their first attempt at a long distance path it is an ideal choice.

Which way should it be walked? The path is blessed with two beginnings and two ends, and if you have the time why not do it each way? I have presented it from south to north for no other reason than personal preference. In that direction, the gentler contours of the south are replaced by the bleaker grandeur of the north; a coast more influenced by the activity of man is exchanged for a more intimate relationship with natural forces. If the weather does happen to be less than ideal, it is more likely to prevail on your back than to drive into your face. Similarly the sun is more often over your shoulder and will enhance the view ahead. In the opposite direction, the walking may be perceived to be less strenuous towards the end and there is possibly greater choice in available accommodation.

The peninsular nature of the coastline makes it equally attractive to the walker who, experiencing constraints through time or capability, is restricted to excursions of more modest proportions. There are many opportunities for circular walks, and a full day's trek on the coast can often be returned by a modest walk along equally delightful inland paths or quiet lanes, but even a return by the outward path will reveal delights missed in the morning. To further help in planning day walks, much of the area is served by public transport. I have included a number of suggestions for day and shorter walks in this guide.

WHEN TO WALK

Presented here as "a walk for all seasons", the decision of when best to undertake the walk is not easily made. Climate and location combine to remove the extreme conditions that could be expected in hill and mountain environments, and ice and snow are rare. However, even though Pembrokeshire lays claim to being the sunniest spot in Wales, it is as susceptible to rain as anywhere else and particularly during the winter months, gale force winds are common. Having said that, fine days in winter can be as equally enjoyable as their summer counterparts, but spring and early summer will give a statistically better chance of fine weather, and the increased hours of daylight can allow the day's walk to be undertaken at a more leisurely pace.

Much will depend on your particular interest; spring starts early and a succession of developing flowers and plants will take the botanist through beyond the summer. Bird watchers will have to decide between the nesting season during the spring and summer and the autumn when migration takes place. Autumn is also the time to observe the seals that arrive at the shores to give birth to their pups; the backdrop of vegetation assumes its rich pre-winter hue and a surprising variety of fungi make their discrete appearance. Even winter is not desolate; in sheltered corners many plants manage to produce flowers, the tidal estuaries attract some winter feeders, and when the winds rise, awe-inspiring waves pound the rocks with an unrepentant fury.

SAFETY PRECAUTIONS

Although not suffering the same dramatic changes of weather conditions and attendant consequence that a mountain expedition would bring, as with any activity a few common-sense considerations will help ensure safety and enjoyment. Always plan your day's walk to be within your capability and allow enough time for its completion. Although the climate is generally mild, wind and rain can combine to test the very best of waterproofs, and although low temperatures in themselves are unlikely to be much of a problem, wind chill can quickly cause enough discomfort to spoil an otherwise enjoyable day. Equally important is protection for the feet and legs. Rough and slippery ground is best tackled in walking boots, and whilst a magnificent job is done in keeping the pathway clear, high gorse and bramble can inflict painful damage on unprotected lower limbs. Equally discomforting is long grass, which manages to retain its wetness long after any rain has passed, and can quickly turn an un-gaitered boot into a foot-bath.

Much of the Path is over high unfenced cliffs and care, particularly with children and dogs, should be taken to avoid obvious dangers. Remain on recognised paths, and do not attempt to climb cliffs or reach "inaccessible" shorelines. Adverse weather conditions can make passage along some sections of the Path dangerous, particularly where narrow unfenced paths skirt precipitous cliffs. Rocks and grass become slippery in the wet, and high blustery winds add to the hazard of falling. Care should also be exercised where there is a risk of landslip and subsidence, particularly after there has been heavy rain; the coastline is constantly changing and in some places, the footpath ever more encroaches onto the bordering fields. Many such places are signed, with minor deviations to the line of the footpath being indicated.

When crossing military firing ranges, use only the marked paths, do not enter any buildings and refrain from touching any ammunition or other objects that may be evident.

On beaches, do not climb cliffs and use only recognised access paths. Many of the convoluted coves have only a single way down and it is important to maintain an awareness of the state of the tide to avoid becoming cut off as the water rises. If you bathe, be aware that many parts of the coast are affected by strong tidal currents and undertows.

A final word for those walkers who are accompanied by their dog. Whilst many dogs would enjoy the prospect of a 290 kilometre "walkies", remember that they, like you, need a degree of fitness to complete the journey in comfort. Some accommodation addresses listed in the guide are happy to accept dogs, but please enquire in advance of your arrival. Many of the farms along the way keep sheep and cattle and the path occasionally lies through or close to a farmyard, so please keep your dog supervised. It has become necessary for reasons of safety and hygiene, particularly in the holiday areas, for the imposition of a prohibition on dogs for part of the year on certain beaches. Information as to which beaches are affected and for what part of the year can be obtained from the local Information Centres.

PLANNING THE WALK

For many people, there is almost as much pleasure to be gained in planning a walk as in actually completing it, and this guide is intended to assist in that process as well as add to your enjoyment along the way. It will hopefully also serve to stimulate your memories of the walk in the years to come and even if you do not keep a daily record of your trip, it is worth remembering to take along a waterproof pen so that you can annotate the margins with your own observations.

The guide describes the route from Amroth to St Dogmael's and includes general comments (in normal type), a route description (in **bold** type) and observations and background information to features or places encountered along the way (in *italic* type). Occasional alternatives or variations to the main route are indented.

Line maps have been included as a guide only, but are, along with the text, probably all that is required for finding the route along the Coast Path. They are not a substitute for the Ordnance Survey maps, which will be necessary for navigation away from the path and for planning your own circular walks, nor do they provide the mass of additional information shown on those maps and which will greatly enhance your enjoyment. The following Ordnance Survey maps cover the area:

1:50,000 Landranger Series (South to North)

Sheet 158 -	Tenby
Sheet 157 -	St David's and Haverfordwest
Sheet 145 -	Cardigan

1:25,000 Pathfinder Series (South to North)

Sheet 1104 (SN 00/10) -	Tenby and Saundersfoot
Sheet 1125 (SN 09/19) -	Manorbier and Tenby
Sheet 1124 (SR 89/99) -	Castlemartin and St Govan's Head
Sheet 1103 (SM 80/90) -	Milford Haven
Sheet 1102 (SM 70) -	Skomer Island
Sheet 1079 (SM 81/91) -	Haverfordwest (Hwlffordd)
Sheet 1055 (SM 62/72) -	St David's (Tyddewi and Ramsey Island)
Sheet 1032 (SM 83/93) -	Fishguard (Abergwaun)
Sheet 1033 (SN 03/13) -	Newport
Sheet 1010 (SN 01/14) -	Cardigan and Dinas Head

1:25,000 Outdoor Leisure Map Series
35   Pembrokeshire North
36   Pembrokeshire South

How long you should allow for the completion of the Coast Path is a purely personal matter. It can be accomplished comfortably within two weeks if you are fit, but there is much of interest along the way, and allowing a little longer will give more time to enjoy the pleasures encountered. There is a need, particularly in the summer months, to book accommodation in advance, but it is well to try to allow for some flexibility and vary the length of each day. If you set targets that leave little time for exploration, watching the birds and waves or even building sand castles and having the odd paddle, you will miss a lot of what the Path has to offer.

With the exception of the circular walks, no attempt has been made in the guide to suggest a distance that should be completed each day. The division into sections is merely for convenience, although in general these do coincide with an availability of accommodation. A table of distances between places where accommodation is available has been included in the Appendices to help in the planning of your own walk.

Besides your own capabilities and the availability of facilities along the route, there are a couple of other points to be taken into consideration in your planning:

Military Ranges - operational use of military firing ranges can result in public access to the coast between Giltar Point (SS 124 983) and Valleyfield Top (SS 109 984), and Broad Haven (SR 977 937) and The Green Bridge (SR 926 946) being temporarily prohibited, and it is then necessary to follow an alternative route. Information regarding intended closure is published in the local press and displayed at local police stations and post offices. Advance information can also be obtained by contacting the camps directly.

Tidal Crossings - passage across two of the river mouths encountered on the route is only possible two hours either side of low tide; arrival at any other time necessitates a wait or substantial detour. These are at Sandy Haven (SM 856 075) and Pickleridge (SM 813 071). The distance between the two points is some 7.75 kilometres (4.8 miles) and could take up to two hours to walk. If possible, therefore, time your arrival at the first crossing to coincide with the

23

falling tide. Occasionally, at very high tides, some difficulty may be experienced for a short time in Angle Bay (SM 877 021 to SM 896 020) as there is no alternative path along the field margin behind the beach and a short wait may be necessary.

Tidal information - tidal information for Milford Haven is published in almanacs and is available at Information Centres in the area. Note that the moment of high tide at other places along the coast does differ from that at Milford, and the variations are published locally.

Transport - Pembrokeshire is easily accessible by road and rail, with services running to Tenby, Pembroke Dock, Milford Haven, Haverfordwest and Fishguard. For people walking on a day basis, the county has an extensive network of public transport that approaches, if not actually meeting, the coastal path at a majority of the villages along its length. Places accessible by local bus service are indicated on the distance table to be found in the Appendices. Services in many areas, however, are infrequent, and walkers using them to complete a day walk should make local enquiries. It is perhaps preferable to use the bus for the outward journey rather than risk an unplanned walk at the end of a long day. Dyfed County Council can provide up-to-date information.

Accommodation - Much of the area is well served with accommodation, although there are one or two sections of the Path where it is separated by a greater than usual distance. It is advisable to book accommodation in advance, particularly during the peak holiday season, although at other times booking ahead may be sufficient to guarantee a bed for the night. A list of accommodation has been included in the Appendices. It is neither comprehensive nor implies any recommendation, but will hopefully assist in planning your days. Some proprietors have indicated that they would be willing to provide parking facilities to long distance walkers or a "collection" service at the end of a day's walk, both at a modest charge. Although not all will be able to provide such services, it is worth enquiring.

The accommodation guide includes a number of campsites and the six youth hostels to be found along the route, some of which also permit camping in their grounds. Walkers intending to camp throughout the route should remember that all land is privately owned and that permission should always be sought before pitching your tent away from a recognised site. Although many farmers will not object, they appreciate being given the chance to say no.

Further information is available from the local Tourist or National Park Information Centres and the Youth Hostel Association.

USEFUL ADDRESSES AND TELEPHONE NUMBERS

Information Officer, Pembrokeshire Coast National Park
County Offices, Haverfordwest, Pembrokeshire,
Dyfed SA61 1QZ (01437) 764591
National Park Information Centre
The Croft,
Tenby (01834) 842402
National Park Information Centre
Harbour Car Park, Saundersfoot (01834) 811411
National Park Information Centre
Drill Hall, Main Street, Pembroke (01646) 682148
National Park Information Centre
National Park Car Park, Broad Haven (01437) 781412
National Park Information Centre
City Hall, St David's (01437) 720392
Fishguard, Goodwick and District Tourist Association
Town Hall, Fishguard (01348) 873612
National Park Information Centre
Long Street, Newport (01239) 820912
Youth Hostel Association
Trevelyan House, 8 St Stephen's Hill, St Albans, Hertfordshire
AL1 2DY (01727) 55215
Dyfed County Council Transport (01267) 224931
Penally Camp (01834) 2358
Castlemartin RAC Camp (01646) 661321

View east over beach from west cliffs, Amroth

Chapter One
AMROTH to TENBY
11.4 kilometres (7.1 miles)

AMROTH

The walk begins, as it ends, in a quiet unassuming village. Each occupies the easternmost coastal limit of the old county of Pembrokeshire; St Dogmael's on the northern coast and Amroth here in the south. Amroth lies in a break within a sweep of cliffs that enclose the north-western corner of Carmarthen Bay. The long, golden strip of shore is backed by a bank of shingle thrown up by winter storm waves. Man has added to this natural defence against the sea, reinforcing it with a concrete sea wall and planting lines of groins out into the sea, as if dividing the beach into seashore gardens for imaginary houses.

When sea levels were lower than today, this countryside was cloaked in a forest that extended far out into what is now the sea and provided hunting grounds for the earliest men who inhabited this coast. When spring tides expose the lower reaches of the beach, blackened petrified stumps of long gone trees are sometimes exposed, and fossilised hazelnuts and pieces of bone, horn and flint artifacts have been found amongst the pebbles on the beach.

At the eastern end of the village, about 0.7 kilometre (0.5 mile) to the north of the coast, evidence of later habitation exists in the form of a banked earthwork. This was a Roman military outpost, thought to have been occupied from around the second to fourth centuries AD. The Norman invasion of Pembrokeshire at the end of the eleventh century brought new settlers to the area. They called the place Earwere and built their own castle overlooking the beach. No trace of it remains and its site is occupied by the present castle. Built in the late eighteenth century, it has now become a holiday centre.

In its more recent history, Amroth was a mining village sustained by a wealth derived from coal and iron ore found in narrow seams that outcrop on the surrounding hillsides. The industry declined in the early years of the twentieth century and much of the evidence for its existence has now disappeared. The village has since developed as a quiet resort, providing for the needs of holidaymakers who come to enjoy its fine, sandy beach and pleasant surrounding countryside.

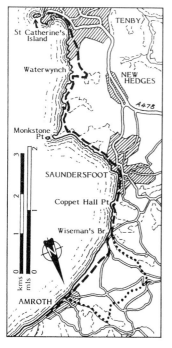

The first kilometres of the walk take you to Saundersfoot and provide a splendid introduction to the Coast Path. The walking is relatively easy, with only one short section of significant climbing, which gives your legs an opportunity to develop a rhythm for the walk ahead. There is much to see as the path alternates between woodland, open cliff top and the margins of the shore. It passes evidence of some of the industrialisation that once imposed a very different countenance on the coast and bordering countryside to that which we see today.

The Coast Path begins at the eastern end of Amroth village. Here, a stream marking the eastern boundaries of Amroth and the old county of Pembrokeshire passes underneath the coastal road before gaining its final freedom in the sea. Fixed to the bridge's squat wall are two brass plaques commemorating the official opening of the Coast Path by Wynford Vaughn Thomas in 1970:

Llwybr Hir
Arfordir Sir Benfro
Traeth Poppit 180 Milltir
Agorwyd Gan
Wynford Vaughn Thomas
1970

Pembrokeshire Coast
Long Distance Footpath
Poppit Sands 180 Miles
Opened by
Wynford Vaughn Thomas
1970

From the bridge, begin by heading west along the road passing Amroth Castle Holiday Park on the way into the village. The decorative crenellations of the castle are just visible behind the grey perimeter wall. Stay with the road until, just beyond a public toilet on the left it is forced inland and upwards by the re-emergence of the cliff line that abruptly marks the end of the village. As it turns to head away from the sea, immediately look for and take a footpath on the left (signposted Coast Path), winding steeply upwards through woodland to reach the top of the cliff.

Part way up, allow yourself the indulgence of a short diversion to a thoughtfully placed seat on a vantage point to the left. From here there is a fine retrospective view over Amroth and its beach, and an early opportunity to develop the ploy: "This might make a good photograph!".

Resume the woodland walk to find that the path soon levels off, emerging from trees to cross a sloping field. Just before the crest of the hill, a stiled gap in the hedgerow to the right gives access to a delightful old track. Cross the stile and follow the track to the left.

Although initially bound by high hedges, the track opens out to allow sight of the shoreline. The sloping cliffs, covered with scrub and gorse, curve ever more steeply to flat rocks and shingle scattered on the beach head below. The path is easy, but often muddy in places. On a sunny day, the overhanging boughs that not infrequently meet, almost forming a tunnel, provide welcome shade.

The western view is most attractive in the highlights of the early morning sun, and gives a foretaste of the delights to come. The sands, punctuated by low bands of rock, sweep underneath high cliffs past Wiseman's Bridge and Saundersfoot to Monkstone Point. Beyond lies Tenby, projecting just far enough into the sea to be seen behind the intervening cliffs, its medieval castle and St Mary's Church visible as silhouettes on the skyline. Lying off the coast adjacent to Tenby is the small island of St Catherine's, and behind it, the much larger Caldey.

In a little under 1 kilometre (0.5 mile) the track meets the end of a narrow metalled lane. Go ahead, past a few houses to the road's end and turn left towards the coast where an inn, The Wiseman's Bridge, overlooks the eastern end of the beach.

WISEMAN'S BRIDGE

Wiseman's Bridge lies at the entrance to the appropriately named Pleasant

Valley. Its marshy bottom, lined with luxuriant tree growth, winds back amongst rolling hills into the surrounding countryside. The beach is a continuation of that at Amroth, with extensive beds of rock breaking out from the sand. Behind it, a bank of shingle carries the road along the shore. The name, as with many places, derives from its one time feudal owner Andrew Wiseman who is recorded as having held land here in 1324.

Coal has been mined since antiquity in the densely wooded valleys that cut into the countryside behind Amroth, Wiseman's Bridge and Saundersfoot. The torrents of water that carved them out of the hillsides exposed thin seams of coal, making it accessible to primitive mining techniques. The coal was won by excavating bell-shaped pits up to 18 metres (60 feet) deep, which were worked to the point of collapse; another would then be started. Evidence remains in the numerous hollows and depressions that can be found hidden amongst the trees and undergrowth that cloak the valley sides.

Although present only in thin seams, the coal, anthracite, was of an exceptional quality and suitable for use in the smelting of iron. Deposits of haematite, an ore of iron, also exist in the surrounding hills and by the nineteenth century the area had become a notable producer of iron ore and iron, as well as coal. Several iron works grew up in the valleys alongside the mines, one being at Stepaside, a small hamlet some 2 kilometres (1.25 miles) to the north of Wiseman's Bridge in Pleasant Valley.

Before the area's industrial heyday, coal had been hauled down Pleasant Valley to the beach by horse and cart, where it was loaded onto boats for transport around the coast. By 1829, the harbour at Saundersfoot had been improved and a tramway was built from Stepaside down the valley to Wiseman's Bridge and then along the coast below the cliffs to Saundersfoot. Steam engines were used to haul the coal and iron to the harbour, where it could be more easily loaded onto the waiting ships.

Iron and coal production is now a memory, but Wiseman's Bridge established its place in modern history when in 1943 Churchill, Montgomery and Eisenhower met here to oversee the rehearsals taking place for Operation Overlord, the prelude to the liberation of Europe.

Walk along the road towards the opposite end of the beach. Just before it begins to climb away from the shore, a path leaves on the left (signposted Coast Path). It leads along a concrete promenade at the base of the crumbling cliffs that rise from the western end of the beach.

A notice warns of the possibility of stone fall from the cliffs above, and a few metres along the promenade a signposted path to the right offers an alternative route over the top of the cliffs.

The coastal route, however, lies ahead along the promenade. It follows the line taken by the old mineral railway that connected Stepaside to Saundersfoot, and passes through two tunnels in the intervening headlands before emerging at a car park behind Coppet Hall.

As you walk below the cliffs, look for two gated adits burrowing into them; haematite was once mined there.

Variant: WISEMAN'S BRIDGE to COPPET HALL via CLIFF TOP

Shortly after leaving the road at Wiseman's Bridge, the variation is signed along a path on the right. Climb steeply through woodland to the top of the cliffs that separate the beaches of Wiseman's Bridge and Saundersfoot. In summer luxuriant vegetation obscures many of the views that would otherwise be offered by the vantage. However, a glimpse back through the trees reveals the curve of Carmarthen Bay stretching towards the Gower peninsula. The path is a pleasing but strenuous alternative. It rejoins the official path at the car park behind Coppet Hall café.

Walk ahead across the car park, passing a telephone box and toilet to leave by another short tunnel which emerges on to the end of The Strand. Follow the street into the centre of Saundersfoot. Alternatively, at low water, you can walk along the beach from Coppet to Saundersfoot.

The Strand was once known as "Railway Street" since the tramway from Stepaside ran along it to the harbour at the other end of the town. One of the town's earliest tourist attractions was the sight of steam engines chugging along the street.

SAUNDERSFOOT

The earliest reference to Saundersfoot by name was made by George Owen in 1603 in a treatise on mining:
"Thys other vayne of coale which I spoke of at Jefreston, acompanieth the second vayne of lymestone on the northe side thereof withyn half a mile of the lymestone and passeth Est to Sanndersfoot and there accompaning the

lymestone to the sea".

The village grew, as did others in the area, as a result of the wealth derived from the mineral extraction from the surrounding hillsides. At first coal, extracted simply from bell mines, was exported from the beach around the coast to Bristol and across the sea to Ireland and France. By the seventeenth century deeper shafts were being sunk, harnessing first water and then later steam power to drain and ventilate the mines and raise the hard won coal to the surface.

Saundersfoot had become a working town and other industries sprang up. Smelting and iron works took advantage of the nearby haematite and limestone to produce both pig and worked iron, and brickyards exploited the local clay to produce firebricks both for export and to build the iron furnaces. By the nineteenth century production had increased sufficiently to justify improving Saundersfoot's harbour and a shipyard soon flourished, servicing the ships that plied in and out of the town. The boom continued until the beginning of this century. However, mining had always been difficult here because the thin seams of coal have suffered much faulting and folding. This, coupled with competition from other coalfields and a reliance on sea transport in an age of developing railways, eventually made mining uneconomic. The collieries and industries which relied upon them fell into decline and the industrial age quietly passed away. The last pit to go, Bonville's Court colliery, finally ceased production in 1938.

At its peak in the mid 1880s, coal, ore and finished iron were exported as far afield as Hong Kong, and annual coal production was in the region of 100,000 tons. Even today it is estimated that some 2 million tons remain in the ground.

Saundersfoot has not shared the fate that many towns experienced when their major industry disappeared. In the years of declining industry, the fashion of seaside holidays became established. Hotels were built to accommodate the families attracted to its fine, sandy beaches, well sheltered from the prevailing winds. The tradition has continued and Saundersfoot remains a pleasant resort.

The wooded valleys around the town still bear traces of its industrial past. Exercise care if walking in the woods and straying from recognised paths, for the old shafts and pits hidden in the undergrowth are unstable and flooded, and can be dangerous. Entry is not recommended.

Climbers in cove east of Proud Giltar

Flimston Bay from east
Thorn Island and West Angle Point

The choice of route through Saundersfoot to the beach below St Bride's Hill on the far side of the harbour depends upon the state of the tide and your inclination. To walk along the beach below Saundersfoot is the most direct, least strenuous and possibly quietest choice. Indeed at low tide it is possible to have walked all the way from Amroth along the beach. However it is rocky for much of the way and as intermediate egress from the beach between Amroth and Saundersfoot is possible only at Wiseman's Bridge and Coppet Hall, sure knowledge of the tide is necessary before departing (see Tidal Information). The rising tide also cuts off the route around the seaward side of Saundersfoot harbour and may cover the small section of beach beyond. In this case a detour along the road over St Bride's Hill will be necessary to rejoin the coast.

Beyond the town, the path follows the contours of the cliffs to Waterwynch, often on the fringe of woodland which grows profusely along this sheltered coast. Although a good path, the walking is strenuous in places where it dips to negotiate the steep valleys that cut through the cliffs.

If it is not high tide, from the end of The Strand cross the car park (where there is an Information Centre) and head for the back of the harbour to go along the walkway that separates it from the sluice on the right.

The sluice was built to retain water at high tide for subsequent release when the level dropped. This scoured the harbour and its entrance of sand, thus keeping it navigable.

Turn left, and follow the quay to the end of the cliffs. Behind the harbour on the right is a ramp to the beach. Walk along the beach for about 250 metres/yards and then leave up a short flight of concrete steps by the side of a stream, to emerge on to a paved road at Rhode Wood.

Before leaving the beach, have a look at the Lady Cave Anticline, to be found at the end of the cliff beyond the stairway. This is a noted geological feature and is a fine example of the extreme folding that has taken place in this area. Compressed layers of sedimentation have been folded upwards into a sharp point. Subsequent erosion of the softer shales at the base has created a small cave in the more resilient sandstone. Exploration of the cliffs along the shore will reveal the thin coal measures in the faulted and folded seams.

Variant: SAUNDERSFOOT to RHODE WOOD via ST BRIDE'S HILL

At high water, it is not possible to walk the short intertidal strip between the harbour and Rhode Wood. You must therefore join the main road (B4316) to the right of the car park and follow it out of the town up St Bride's Hill (signposted Tenby). Part way up, a gap in the hedge allows a postcard view over the harbour, the coast sweeping back beyond Amroth. At the top of the hill, past the St Brides Hotel, take the second of two roads on the left, The Glen (signposted Coast Path). Walk through a small housing development to the bottom of the hill to meet the path coming from the beach.

From the beach, turn left into Rhode Wood (signposted Coast Path) and follow a track that twists upwards through a delightful old woodland of small twisted oak trees whose branches form a canopy over the carpet of plants covering its floor.

There are ample diversions for botanists and amateurs alike in the many species of flora that thrive throughout the year. The extensive woodland in this area is a contrast to much of what will be experienced later on. Its easterly aspect substantially protects it from the stunting effects of salt spray, whipped from the sea by the prevailing south-westerly winds that affect most of the Pembroke coast.

The track passes over cliff tops, in places running along the edge of sheer cliffs from which there are splendid panoramic views over Carmarthen Bay. Eventually, descend almost to sea level into the first of three wooded valleys breaking the cliffs between Saundersfoot and Tenby, where there is safe access to the beach. The way onward lies ahead, across a plank bridge and up the steep hillside opposite.

Remnants of the industrial activity that the subterranean wealth attracted to the area now lie hidden amongst the trees. To the right, as the path climbs away from the stream, is a limekiln and a little further on are some deep depressions and holes; all that remain of old mine shafts. At the top, the woodland clears to expose steeply sloping cliffs, thick with gorse and bracken, sweeping to the rocks and narrow beach below.

Approaching Monkstone Point, the prominent headland seen from Amroth, the track undulates through a larch wood. A path on the left runs along its northern flank to return some 100 metres/

yards further on, where another path (signposted) drops to the beach below Monkstone Point's southern slopes.

On a fine day, the clarity of the water washing over the golden sand and rocks below adopts an almost tropical brilliance. If you go down to the beach, keep to the marked track as the steeply inclined shales can be unstable.

Beyond Monkstone Point, the path stays high above the beach, alternating between field margins and sloping cliffs. Shortly after passing a lookout point and transmitter mast, leave the fields and drop steeply through a conifer plantation into Lodge Valley. A more gradual climb takes the path on to Waterwynch.

Lodge Valley is a delightful spot; in spring its wooded flanks display subtle hues of green and have an air of poetic remoteness that is a visual foil for the ever-steepening cliffs extending towards Tenby.

Above Waterwynch, the path turns inland along the valley, gently losing height beside a fringe of woodland. After crossing a small stream, it drops left over another bridge and then across a stile to reach a metalled drive leading to Waterwynch House Hotel. Cross the drive to another stile (signposted Coast Path, and Beach), a few metres beyond the track divides, the Coast Path turning right up Waterwynch Lane, an attractive track that takes the route over the final hill to Tenby.

The uphill section of Waterwynch Lane has been paved with concrete lattice, so although steep, the climb is relatively easy. When descending the opposite side of the hill, choose the left of the two parallel paths; its concrete steps being preferable to the often muddy path to the right.

On the descent, the path passes Allen's View, a local viewpoint dedicated to the memory of one Jessie Allen. Its northern aspect gives an unobstructed view back along the coast, but that overlooking Tenby is partly obscured by trees.

Waterwynch Lane finally meets civilisation just past a caravan site where it becomes The Croft, a marine drive high above Tenby North Beach leading to the town. At the end of The Croft on the right is an Information Centre.

The Victorian terrace at the far end of The Croft, its row of private gardens perched on top of the cliffs just below the road, is sited to take full advantage of the view across the bay to the harbour, lifeboat station and castle. It symbolises the elegance of the town's development as an early tourist resort.

Chapter Two

TENBY to STACKPOLE QUAY

23.4 kilometres (14.5 miles)

TENBY

The Welsh name for Tenby, Dinbych-y-Pysgod, The Little Fort of the Fishes, aptly summarises the town's early history. There may well have been a settlement here much earlier, but it is first described in the eighth century as a Viking fishing settlement. In the next century, an anonymous poet referred to "the fine fortress over the sea", the fortress no doubt being necessary to defend the prosperity created by herring fishing and trade from marauding opportunists plundering the coasts. Norman conquerors arrived towards the end of the eleventh century and established their presence with a castle on the rocky promontory overlooking the town, although little remains of it today. However, security remained elusive, and the town was sacked on at least two occasions by the Welsh in the ensuing 200 years. In 1328 Edward III granted rights to levy taxes on the port's trade to build a breakwater for the harbour and to maintain the town's walls. They were strengthened in 1457 and again in 1588 in anticipation of attack by the Spaniards. A plaque inscribed "1588 E.R.30" in the wall just south of the South West Gate commemorates the work done. A significant portion of the western wall still stands alongside St Florence and South Parades.

The town's turbulent history continued; Henry Earl of Richmond, subsequently Henry VII, sought refuge here on his escape to Brittany following the Battle of Tewksbury in 1471. Two centuries later the town was vigorously contended by both sides during the Civil Wars and between 1643 and 1648 was attacked several times from both land and sea. In 1869 a fort was erected on St Catherine's Island opposite Castle Hill as an outlying part of the Milford Haven defences.

The town's political importance no doubt reflected its economic influence within Pembrokeshire. By Norman times it rivalled Pembroke and Haverfordwest as the principal trading and fishing port of the region, a prominence that it maintained into the Industrial Age, when its trading ships helped satisfy the increasing demand for Pembrokeshire's coal. At the end of the eighteenth century, the town became popular as a seaside spa,

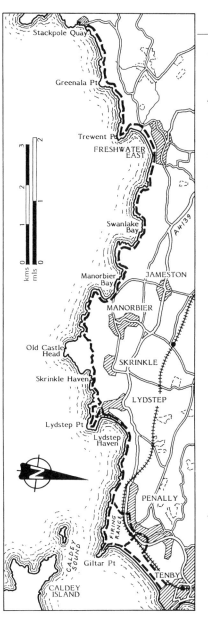

developing a reputation for its favourable climate and "waters" - the sea. To cater for an ever increasing number of visitors, the town was "modernised", with improvements to the streets, buildings and other facilities, which included the installation of a proper water supply. Much of the work was conceived by William Paxton, a Carmarthenshire landowner, who had made his fortune in India. It is largely his town we see today. Many of the guest houses and hotels, built to accommodate Georgian and Victorian visitors, still exist. The best were strategically lined along the high limestone cliffs to take full advantage of splendid sea views.

The coming of the railways signalled the end of the coastal trade, but Tenby's new future was already secure. The railway's arrival in the town in 1856 brought with it an increasing number of holidaymakers, and the trading ships that had previously filled the harbour were replaced by pleasure boats, which entertained their patrons with cruises in the Bristol Channel. Since then, the town has adapted well to

37

meet the changing fashions of the British Holiday and has retained much of the character that established its popularity.

As at Saundersfoot, the choice of route will depend upon need and inclination; my suggested route through the town passes a number of its historical sites, although you may, if the tide is out, go down to the beach opposite St Catherine's Island and walk below the South Cliff.

At the end of The Croft opposite the Tourist Information Centre, go left down a flight of steps to the lower promenade and walk on to the harbour.

The harbour retains much of its old-world charm, nestling below the crook of Castle Hill. The surrounding mélange of buildings, many instigated by Paxton, create a casual elegance overlooking the flock of little boats that move in and out on the summer tides. The sluice behind the harbour dates from the early seventeenth century, and marked a resurgence of the port's prosperity. It serves the same purpose as that at Saundersfoot: to help keep the harbour navigable. Further improvements were made in the following decades, with the building of the South Wharf in 1763 and in 1842, the replacement of the medieval quay, which had served the harbour for over five hundred years, by the present stone pier. The tall building at the corner of the sluice, now accommodating Tenby Sailing Club, was a warehouse to hold imported wine.

Many landings along the Pembroke coast are associated with early Celtic Christian tradition, and chapels were often built close by. At Tenby the dedication was to St Julian the Hospitaller, patron of boatmen, and a chapel was first established in the sixth century. It has long since disappeared. A later chapel stood on the end of the medieval pier. Before its demolition it had fallen into secular use, becoming the town's first seawater baths and subsequently a blacksmith's forge. The present chapel, passed as you leave the harbour, was erected in 1870. The building behind the chapel was constructed in 1874 to provide accommodation for seamen. It is now divided into flats, but notice that the names above the doors still preserve its maritime association.

Walk from the harbour past St Julian's Chapel. At the top, bear left into Castle Square and leave it at its far end through an opening on the right of Laston House. The path circles the seaward side of Castle Hill, returning you to the entrance of Castle Square.

Variant: TENBY SOUTH BEACH

If you wish to avoid the town and the tide is out (see Tidal Information), go down to the beach on the south side of Castle Hill. Follow the base of South Cliff to the café at its far end.

At the end of Castle Square above the harbour stands Laston House. One of William Paxton's elegant buildings, it was constructed in 1811 to house the seawater baths. The apposite Greek quotation from Euripides inscribed above the door, translated as "The sea washes away all the ills of mankind", has been adopted as the town's motto.

The first Lifeboat station was established in 1852 by the Shipwrecked Mariners' Society and handed to the RNLI two years later. The courage of the sailors who have manned the eight lifeboats stationed here since that time is reflected in the 450 lives saved by their efforts. Local support has always been important, but in 1897 a head launcher had to be appointed with the specific duty of limiting the number of helpers at a launch to 50. An investigation the previous year had counted as many as 106 willing hands turning up to assist at a launch; eight years later, it was decided to further reduce the number to four for safety reasons.

Little remains of the Norman castle that surmounted the rocky promontory above the harbour, although its strategic importance can be appreciated in the fine view from the summit. A large marble memorial there honours Prince Albert, consort to Queen Victoria, its first stone being laid by George White, the then mayor of Tenby, on the third anniversary of the Prince's death. The mounted cannon nearby were originally used for the defence of the town and date from the seventeenth century. On the southern side of the hill, housed in one of the old castle buildings, is the town's small but interesting museum.

The fort on St Catherine's Island opposite is contemporary with those defending the Milford Haven waterway. It was built in 1869 on the site of a chapel dedicated to St Catherine, patron saint of spinners, a trade that was carried out in the town until the sixteenth century. The threatened French invasion never materialised and its garrison of 60 men and heavy armament were never required to fire "a shot in anger". There is no public access to it.

From Castle Square, walk ahead along Bridge Street to the Merchant's House, facing you at its far end.

Dating from the late fifteenth century, the Tudor Merchant's House and its neighbour, Plantagenet House, are well-preserved examples of Tudor architecture. The Merchant's House was given by the town Corporation to the National Trust in 1937, and is open during the summer. It is furnished to depict the lifestyle that a prosperous merchant of the time might have enjoyed.

Turn left in front of the Merchant's House, emerging from the passageway into Tudor Square. Go right to St Mary's Church and pass it on the left into St George's Street (the entrance to the church, however, is from High Street to the right of the church).

St Mary's Church dominates Tudor Square and dates from at least the thirteenth century. The church, like the town, has seen many changes and has gradually grown from a simple building, of which few traces remain, into the magnificent church of today. The present structure was largely conceived in the fifteenth century, and is the largest church in Pembrokeshire, except for the cathedral at St David's. Its splendid architecture is matched by an elegant interior, which embodies features associated with Somerset and Devon; close neighbours at a time when the most convenient communication was by sea. Particularly notable is the "wagon" roof over the long chancel which was built around 1470. Magnificent carvings on its bosses, most dating from that period, depict a variety of subjects; intriguing mythical and grotesque creatures, fishes and leaves complement the Four Evangelists and other religious symbols. The wall-posts supporting the roof are carved as robed figures each holding shields. The surrounding chapels and walls contain effigies and monuments, remembering people who have contributed to the life and history of the town.

The church has not been immune from the destruction suffered by the rest of the town over the years. The local Elizabethan writer George Owen wrote of the church's destruction in 1187 by a band of Welshmen led by Maelgwn. Local tradition attributes the damage to the figure of William Risam, a merchant and former Mayor, on the east wall of St Thomas' Chapel, to a musketeer under Cromwell who mistook the figure for a man. In 1842, a cannon-ball, thought to have been fired during Cromwell's siege of the town, was discovered in the roof above the choir.

St George's Street leads out of the old town through The Five Arches, where you should turn left into St Florence Parade and walk alongside the wall to South Cliff. Turn right and at the end of the Esplanade drop to the café on the beach below.

The impressive remaining section of the town wall includes the only surviving gate, known as The Five Arches. The other gates fell to Paxton's expansionary developments in the eighteenth century. Outside the gate is a plaque commemorating the success of Doctor Charter in securing a High Court action in 1873 to prevent further demolition of the walls.

The route to Skrinkle Haven is clear and is an easy walk. The high south facing limestone cliffs beyond Giltar provide excellent views across the sound to Caldey and are a dramatic contrast to the coal measures and grits which underlay the path from Amroth. A level and more open grassy plateau replaces undulating shrubs and woodlands. The cliffs too are different; the effects of erosion have created cleaner lines and there is less confusion in the rock structure. It is a foretaste of the more extensive limestone formations that will be encountered later between Stackpole and Linney Head.

When firing is taking place on Penally Rifle Range, the coast between Giltar Point and Valleyfield Top is closed and you must detour via the main road at Penally (see route variation). Red flags are flown from the top of the cliffs and at the entrance to the range at Penally to indicate closure (See Range Information). However if you are feeling energetic, it is worth climbing onto Giltar Point to enjoy the view before returning to the beach and then following the alternative route.

Walk away from the café along the beach to the foot of Giltar Point ahead. Leave the shore at the far end by a flight of wooden steps (signposted Coast Path). The path then climbs left through bracken and grass onto the tip of the headland. Keep to the path to minimise erosion of the fragile dune system.

Variant: TENBY to VALLEYFIELD TOP

If you wish to avoid both the beach and Giltar Point, after dropping from the Esplanade go away from the beach past a car park behind the café along a track (signposted Coast Path). On reaching a railway embankment, turn left (again signposted Coast Path). Follow a path alongside the track until forced right through a kissing gate and across the railway line. Continue ahead along a gravel drive to the main road and there turn left. Walk past Penally railway station and follow the remaining instructions detailed in the Variant describing the route from the South Beach to Valleyfield.

Almost 2 kilometres of beach stretch ahead, the scene dominated by the flat topped peninsula of Giltar Point and Caldey Island. At low water, the firm sand is littered with a variety of shells, pebbles of all colours and textures and other seaborne curiosities, and provides yet another distraction to impede hasty progress. Old quarries below the path onto Giltar were exploited for limestone, which was loaded directly onto waiting boats for transport around the coast. It was then burnt and spread as lime on the fields.

From the headland there is a superb view of Tenby, its elegant buildings clustered around Castle Hill. St Catherine's Island is pierced by a sea cave, clearly visible from this angle. The flat land behind the sand dunes was the once navigable tidal estuary of the Rhydeg. In medieval times boats sailed up the river as far as St Florence, but accretion of sand dunes led to the silting up of the river mouth. Land reclamation hastened the process, culminating in the construction of an embankment to carry the railway into the town in 1811. Tradition accords Penally, over to the left, as being the birthplace of St Teilo. Excavations in a cave at Longbury Bank, overlooking the Rhydeg Valley, discovered fragments of pottery and human remains and have led to speculation that it may have been a hermit's cell. It is also believed that a monastery existed in the vicinity.

CALDEY ISLAND

Caldey derives from the Norse meaning Cold Island, which is perhaps less inviting than its Welsh name of Ynys Byr, the Island of Byr. As with virtually all the islands around the coast, there is an early Christian tradition. The earliest Celtic settlement on the island was founded by a hermit, St Pyro (Byr), who was drowned in 521. He was succeeded as its abbot by Samson, a contemporary of Teilo, and David who later became Bishop of Dol in Brittany.

With the arrival of the Normans, the island was included in the lands given to Robert Fitz-Martin, whose father had played a prominent role in the conquest of Pembrokeshire. He had already established an abbey at St Dogmael's, and in 1133 his family gave Caldey to monks of the same Order, Benedictines from Tiron in France. The religious settlement continued until the Dissolution in 1534 when the island passed through a succession of secular ownerships before being bought in 1906 by Benjamin Carlyle, the founder of an Anglican Benedictine Brotherhood. He was responsible for most of today's buildings. In 1913 the Order was received into the Roman church but support for it waned, the monks eventually leaving for Prinknash *in Gloucestershire. In 1929 the Benedictines sold the island to Cistercians from Chimay in Belgium. Today, their small community support themselves by farming and the sale of a perfume that they make from the island's flowers.*

Caldey can be visited by boat from Tenby. Although access on the island is limited, there is a splendid beach and it is possible to walk to the lighthouse above the southern cliffs. There are three churches to visit, their names remembering early saints: St Samson, St David and St Illtyd. The monastery can also be visited, but only by men.

Almost detached from Caldey at low tide is St Margaret's Island. The island was extensively quarried for limestone until the last century, and the ruins on top are said to be the quarrymen's cottages. It is now a bird reserve run by the West Wales Naturalists' Trust and is an important breeding site for cormorants and guillemots.

From the tip of Giltar there is a last glimpse of Amroth, and to the west, 16 kilometres (10 miles) away by crow but much further by foot, is the promontory of St Govan. Closer are the more immediate objectives of Lydstep and Old Castle Head.

Follow the path west through long grass towards a lonely stile, whose abutting fence has long since disappeared; it still serves to mark the line of the path. Continue ahead, along the cliff tops, the path gently undulating over a grassy limestone heath to Valleyfield Top, which marks the western limit of the range. However if the range is in use you must instead return to the beach and follow the alternative route.

Variant: TENBY SOUTH BEACH to VALLEYFIELD TOP

About 300 metres/yards from the south-western end of the beach, a path (identified by a notice warning of the dangers of White Bank, an offshore sandbank) leads over the dunes and golf course, passing the foot of the rifle range and crossing the railway, to emerge on the road beside Penally railway station. Walk left along the road for about 0.6 kilometre (0.3 mile) to a track on the left (signposted Coast Path). This goes underneath the railway to a stile. Once over, follow the right hand fence line (again signposted Coast Path) to rejoin the Coast Path at a sentry box on Valleyfield Top.

From Valleyfield Top the route is west over Proud Giltar, the

highest feature along this stretch of coast, before dropping back to the beach at Lydstep Haven.

A wall of impressive limestone stretches ahead, leaning steeply to buttress the land above the sea. Even on a calm day white flecked waves incessantly worry its base, searching for weakness and opportunity. Notice in the cliffs at the back of Sandtop Bay, on the western side of Caldey, a distinct vertical line marking the transition between the limestone (on which you are standing) and the Old Red Sandstone. You will cross that same geological division further along the coast. Sandstone is evident on the hillside behind Penally where, after ploughing, rich red soil covers the fields before they have had time to recover their greenery.

Not far from the range boundary, above Beck's Bay, is an impressive blowhole, its base connected to the sea by a cave through the separating cliff. There is another, equally as dramatic, a little further on. Just before the crest of Proud Giltar, beside the path on the left, is a fine example of a small limekiln. It was purposely built into the side of the rising hill, to facilitate its charging with limestone and the subsequent removal of the burnt lime from the bottom. Of the many that you will pass along the coast, this one is unusual in that it is built on the top of the cliff rather than on the shore.

Once past Proud Giltar, Lydstep Haven comes fully into view, the wide sweep of its sandy bay sheltered by cliffs on either side. It was once the home of the first Viscount of St David's and was described in 1886 as a Sweet little Cove, and indeed it has an almost perfect setting. However, the natural beauty that prompted those words has surrendered to holiday development. Terraces of caravans now line the hillside behind the shore, each jostling for its obligatory sea view.

The Coast Path follows the high water line along the beach below the holiday site towards the towering cliffs of Lydstep Head at the far side.

LYDSTEP

An observant eye comparing the cliffs on either side of the bay will notice that the bay lies in the base of a syncline or downfold in the strata, and the dip is in opposing directions on either side, meeting below the sea. Erosion of the overlying rocks has subsequently created the bay. As at Giltar Point, the cliffs below Lydstep were also quarried for their limestone. The masonry blocks which lie at the base of the cliffs enclosing the southern end of the bay are all that now remain of a quay from which the stone was loaded onto waiting cargo ships.

Leave the beach at its far end, (signposted Coast Path) and follow the site road through a gateway to Lydstep Point. At the top of the hill beside the entrance to a National Trust car park, the Coast Path is signed half left through a gate. However that would deprive you of a tour of the headland, so instead turn sharp left into the car park and then left again, picking up a path through woodland to rejoin the cliff edge. Follow the cliff path around the promontory.

On a clear day there is a splendid panorama, with views east past Caldey to Worms Head on the other side of Carmarthen Bay and south across the Bristol Channel to Lundy. Westwards along the coast past Skrinkle Haven and Old Castle Head, the ruddy cliffs of sandstone are a contrast to the grey of those below your feet.

On the southern side of the headland, dramatic formations are revealed. The sedimentary layers forming the rock have been tilted to rise almost vertically from the sea, and run parallel to the cliff edge. The waves in exploiting weaknesses have broken through the outer wall to scoop out the dramatic basin of Mother Carey's Kitchen and the famous Lydstep caverns at the back of the bay ahead. Below the path at the western end of the head is a funnel shaped blowhole connecting to the sea by a cave, aptly named Smugglers Cave; it is best seen from the opposite side of the valley as you climb away from Lydstep. The rock formations and caves in the cliffs around the rocky inlet below are worthy of exploration, and can be reached at low tide.

The headland path rejoins the signed Coast Path where a flight of steps (signposted Coast Path and Caverns) leads down to the gorge, the path climbing steeply out on the opposite side. A clear route then leads above Skomer Bay and over Horseback, the site of former coastal defences, towards Skrinkle Haven.

The path between Lydstep Gorge and Skrinkle was only acquired by the National Park in 1983, following its release from military use as a gunnery school since the Second World War. During the First World War it had been used as a base for airships engaged in submarine search. Today there is free access to this beauty spot and some of the remaining military buildings have been converted into a youth hostel. The headland, through lack of management, has been colonised by thick gorse and scrub that previous grazing would have kept clear and allowed space for a profusion of wild flowers. The National Park is reintroducing grazing to recreate the short turf, a habitat which would, amongst other things, favour the return of the chough, now increasing in numbers along some parts of the Pembrokeshire coast.

Approaching Skrinkle the path diverts inland to avoid a sewage works, continuing along its access road to a car park. However, you should head back to the cliffs by taking a path on the left immediately after the sewage compound, to see the Beach at Skrinkle.

SKRINKLE HAVEN

Skrinkle Haven is split into three adjacent bays at the foot of perpendicular cliffs. There is access to the middle and most westerly coves down steep staircases situated either side of the sewage works. Although a long way down, at low tide it is worth the effort of the return climb to explore the shore. The eastern steps are easier to climb, so I would suggest descending by those to the west of the sewage works. The beach is strewn with boulders of sandstone, conglomerate and limestone, and the division between the limestone and Old Red Sandstone is clearly visible in the vertical strata at the back of the bay. A massive tongue of rock projects from the cliffs to form the eastern wall of this cove, and in it, two adjacent caves connect with a lateral chamber; these are known as the Church Doors. To the right is a much smaller arch which leads through to the central cove. Although readily visible from the west, it is less so from the east but can be clearly seen from near the base of the steps into the central cove. Through the eastern wall of this cove is an arch of cathedralic proportions cutting through into the final tiny cove. Its base is flooded and all but the most agile will get their feet wet. However when the tide is well out there is access around the foot of the tongue. Be careful not to get cut off by the tide in this final cove; there is no access out onto the cliffs.

The Coast Path leaves the cliffs at Skrinkle for about 0.75 kilometre (0.5 mile) to pass the Royal Armoured Corps Manorbier Camp, which occupies Old Castle Head. It then rejoins the coast, following it to Manorbier Bay.

Return to the car park and pass through to the road. Turn left and then right, passing the main gateway to the camp. Immediately after it, cross a stile on the left (signposted Coast Path) into a field and walk ahead. The route is waymarked and follows the camp perimeter fence, eventually returning to the cliffs above Presipe Bay.

Vertical sandstone beds rising out of the sea form the cliffs of Old Castle

Beach at Skrinkle Haven

Head, now to your left. The scattered buildings and stark wire fences of today's modern military presence are a far cry from the low huts that once housed the Iron Age defenders of the same headland. To the west, the coast sweeps on to Stackpole and St Govan's Head some 10 kilometres (6.2 miles) away. Distant angular headlands of grey limestone contrast with the more rounded sandstone formations of the intervening coast.

Walk above Presipe Bay and on to Priest's Nose where the path turns in to drop to the head of the beach in Manorbier Bay.

Just below the path west of Presipe is a curious hole in the rock, just big enough for a couple of people to crawl into. A romantic imagination can suggest a number of possibilities as to its origin, but the truth is more prosaic: it is thought to have been started as a schoolboy's den and subsequently enlarged by inquisitive travellers.

Beyond, vertical beds of sandstone run parallel to the line of the coast in a curious fashion towards Priest's Nose. The Nose is dramatically split by vertical chasms cutting through the cliffs below, meeting the very edge of the path. Their depth is emphasised by the narrowness and almost mechanical precision with which their excavation appears to have been undertaken. Just beyond is a Neolithic burial chamber, dated to 3,000 BC and known as Kings

Quoit. The large capstone was originally supported on three upright stones, and although one has fallen it remains an impressive monument. The wall of similar slabs behind it at first sight appears to be part of the monument; it is a natural outcrop of vertically layered rock. The slabs for the dolmen were taken from it.

MANORBIER

Manorbier Castle was in 1145 the birth place of Giraldus Cambrensis, Gerald of Wales, a tall and, in his youth, reputedly handsome man. He was the son of a Norman knight, William de Barri, the name taken from Barry Island off the Glamorgan Coast. Encouraged by his father and uncle to enter the church, he studied at the Benedictine abbey of St Peter in Gloucester before going to St David's. An ambitious man, Giraldus had a dream to be appointed the Bishop of St David's and free the church in Wales from subservience to Canterbury. On the death in 1176 of his uncle, the then Bishop of St David's, Giraldus received support for his cause. However, King Henry II perhaps saw in this a platform from which Welsh Nationalism might develop and would not confirm his appointment. On the death of the succeeding Bishop, he was again recommended, this time to King Richard I. The King died before reaching a decision, and although his successor John appeared to show private support he would not make an announcement. Giraldus' spiritual brothers at St David's who had proposed him suggested that he travel to Rome to appeal directly to the Pope, Innocent III. He too was indecisive and Giraldus spent the next four years there, arguing his case. Eventually, poverty and despondency forced him to return home to renew his protest to the King against the appointment of the other nominees. However, his misfortunes continued and he was imprisoned in France, then at war with England. He was eventually released and met King John at Elbeuf, where he denounced the other three nominees put forward as being either illiterate, a bastard or fornicator. The King remained undecided and Giraldus returned to England, where he made a final appeal to the Archbishop of Canterbury. In the end all his petitions were fruitless and an Englishman, Geoffrey de Henelawe, was finally appointed.

He had been offered bishoprics in Ireland and elsewhere in Wales, but it was that of St David's that he wanted. Following these rejections, Giraldus' zeal waned and he spent the remaining years until his death in 1223 writing. His prolific legacy provides many insights and amusing anecdotes of the life of the period, albeit some erring on the fanciful. Perhaps his best known compositions are his descriptions of Wales and of a journey through Wales, which he undertook in 1188 in the company of Baldwin, the Archbishop of Canterbury.

He refers to his birthplace as the house of Pyrrus (Byr or Barri), his father's name, and describes it as a fortified mansion on a hill, close to the sea, and reaching to a harbour on its western side. It was surrounded by orchards through which a stream ran, powering a mill. Unashamedly, he speaks of the land of his genesis as being the best in the whole of Wales.

The castle, a short walk from the beach, was built around 1130 and remains a substantial building worthy of inspection. Before reaching the castle, a track on the left leads past the mill, its walls still standing. Inside, lying on the floor, is the substantial shaft of the old wheel, half hidden in lush vegetation. Beyond, past a discreetly screened sewage works, a wonderfully preserved dovecote hides behind the trees. A circular tower, its roof is corbelled to a dome that is pierced in the centre, no doubt to allow the ingress and egress of its tenants. Inside there are neat rows of nest boxes encircling the walls. It is a sight not to be missed. Overlooking the castle from the opposite hillside is the square towered church of St James.

The coast has so far retained a pastoral quality, bordering a gentle and often wooded countryside. To the west it adopts a more rugged and predominantly open aspect. The way becomes more taxing, particularly beyond Freshwater East, as erosion by the sea and streams compete with an already undulating coastline to create extreme variations in the height of the path above the sea. The reasons for these changes lie in the weathering properties of the rock, Old Red Sandstone, and the fact that the coast generally faces the prevailing winds. It is a fine and dramatic walk along broken cliffs, their base lined with chaotic debris. A greater feeling of remoteness is experienced, perhaps heightened by there being no inland access between Freshwater East and Stackpole.

Cross the beach and leave its northern corner, making for the road at a small layby. There, a path on the left (signposted Coast Path) follows the coast, past a low cottage, The Dak. At the western end of the bay, the path climbs above East Moor Cliff before reverting to the beach in the sheltered bay of Swanlake.

Although lacking height there is plenty to captivate interest. Deep fissures cut across the strata below the path and become more impressive towards the western end of Manorbier Bay. Tilted almost to the vertical, the layers of sandstone underfoot run in ridges parallel with the coast. The path onto East Moor follows such a ridge. At the point of turning into Swanlake, weathered protrusions of the ridges to the right of the path almost give the appearance of an Iron Age fort.

Swanlake, like Manorbier, is hidden from view until the path actually turns into the bay. It is a delightful place, and its splendid beach, ideally placed to capture the afternoon sun, can often be enjoyed in solitude.

The onward path skirts the rocks behind the bay before climbing to West Moor Cliff. There, an easy path across open heathland leads to Freshwater East, where it drops to dunes at the back of the beach. Tired legs may prefer to walk along the firmer sand of the beach. As the dunes are suffering the effects of too many feet, cross them only on marked tracks.

Freshwater East, with its fine sandy beach, became popular at the end of the 1930s as a holiday retreat. With no regulation to planning, many people built their "cottage by the sea" on the tree covered hillside above the beach. They remain today in various states of repair, a monument to prewar middle class life. More recent attempts to revive the beach's popularity as a resort have resulted in the construction of a holiday complex in the base of the valley feeding the bay.

Leave the beach for the road and turn left. A few metres/yards on, leave to the left (signposted Coast Path) along a gravel drive to a public slipway. Pass the slipway (again signposted Coast Path) to a stile and cross into a field. A path then climbs half left to the crest of Trewent Point.

At the top, a track loops to the left around the Point. The promontory progressively narrows towards its end and the exploitation of weaknesses in its southern cliffs has created a wild and rugged scene that dramatically contrasts with the gentle sweep of Freshwater behind.

Rejoin the main path and follow it along the rim of cliffs that stretch, ever increasing in height, towards Greenala Point ahead. There are several stretches of strenuous climbing before its summit is finally reached.

The weathering of the intervening cliffs is spectacular. Massive chunks of rock stand detached from the main cliffs. Boulders lie precariously poised on shelving ledges, awaiting a final impetus before completing their destructive journey to join the chaotic debris below. The defences of the Iron Age fort crowning the summit of Greenala are particularly impressive. A series of

Stack displaying down-fold at Stackpole

deep ditches and high banks defend its landward approach, and are prominent on the skyline from afar. The impression of impregnability is enhanced as you complete the climb to the top. Any but the most determined attempt at invasion would probably have faded half way up because of "lack of puff". Before leaving, walk onto the tip of the promontory for a spectacular retrospective view to Trewent. Ahead lies the contrasting limestone scenery of Stackpole, the Head rising dramatically from the waves and planed flat by the seas of an earlier geological era. Notice that its extremity is pierced by a massive sea cave.

Beyond Greenala, the path continues to climb, albeit more gently, before again meeting the beach at Stackpole Quay.

Stackpole marks the return to limestone, and the division is clearly visible in the back of a small square bay just to the north of Stackpole Quay. As if to emphasise the new geology, a small blowhole lies beside the path a little further on. Dominating the centre of the bay just beyond is a much weathered stack, its mille feuille layering vividly illustrating the folding to which these ancient rocks have been subjected.

Limekiln above Stackpole Harbour

Chapter Three
STACKPOLE QUAY to FRESHWATER WEST
20.8 kilometres (12.9 miles)

STACKPOLE

Stackpole Quay lies in an inlet between two low protecting headlands, the northern of which provides an excellent view of the tiny harbour. Its natural assets have been enhanced by a massive squat jetty extending from an old quarry beneath the cliffs forming its southern wall. The quay was built towards the end of the eighteenth century to facilitate the landing of coal, needed to heat Stackpole Court. The departing boats took away with them cargoes of limestone. There is a fine limekiln standing at the side of the road behind the beach; this was used to manufacture lime for the estate farm.

Stackpole derives its name from the Norse "Stac", meaning an isolated rock, and "Pollr", a small inlet; this suggests that Viking adventurers visited the place. The Normans certainly settled here, and an eleventh century castle built by Elidur de Stackpole is known to have existed. By the middle of the seventeenth century an estate was held by the Lort family, and in 1689 Elizabeth Lort married Alexander Campbell, heir to his family's seat at Cawdor, which overlooks the Murray Firth in Scotland. She inherited the Stackpole estate on her brother's death, and thus it passed into the Campbell family, who were responsible for building the last great house, Stackpole Court, in 1735. The house survived until 1963 when it was demolished by the fifth Earl of Cawdor. On his death in 1970 some 2,000 acres of the estate passed into the ownership of the National Trust.

This south-western corner of Pembrokeshire is almost entirely composed of limestone. It is a massive and relatively level, square shaped headland that presents its face directly towards the prevailing south-westerly winds. In consequence the vegetation along the coast is markedly different to that previously encountered. Well drained soils and continual salt laden winds discourage the growth of trees. In their place are grass and gorse covered heaths from which spring a multitude of lovely flowers. Particularly in spring, the cliffs are delicately tinted with masses of pastel coloured flowers, bobbing in the breeze.

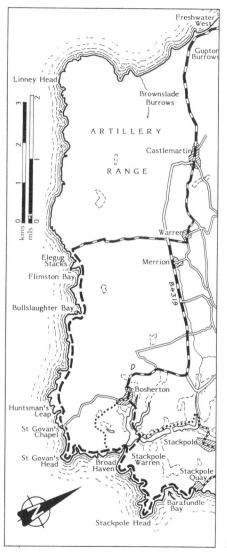

Ahead lies some of the most impressive coastal limestone scenery in Britain. Walking is easy, the path dropping to the beach only at Barafundle and again at Broad Haven, but otherwise running on top of almost horizontal limestone cliffs. There are excellent view points for the many geological features along the way, and during spring and summer the cliffs and offshore stacks provide nesting places for thousands of seabirds.

A flight of steps leads off the beach at Stackpole through a gap in a stone wall onto the headland. A clear path crosses the down to the cliffs above Barafundle Bay.

There is much to appreciate in the blowholes, fissures and sea caves that spectacularly sunder these headlands. This area must have been a particular favourite of the Lort family as their name is preserved in features on either side of

Mowingword cliffs on Stackpole Head

Barafundle Bay. The peregrinations of the cliff provide a more interesting route than the obvious straight track across the grass. Take care, particularly in windy conditions; it is a long way down and people don't always bounce too well!

An arched gateway on the cliffs above Barafundle marks the top of a stone staircase descending to the beach, a legacy of the Cawdor estate. The path away on the far side is less grand, and climbs through a small copse of sycamore, growing in the shelter offered by the cliffs, to the headland behind. Ignore any temptation to cut across the Warren, but follow, with care, the airy route around its perimeter.

The complexities of the coastline are illustrated by the retrospective view. Grey precision of the immediate cliffs contrasts with the more rolling and chaotic band of those reaching back to Trewent. The scenery below, particularly on the southern side of the headland, is nothing short of magnificent. Penetrated by a cave, the tip of the headland is connected by a natural bridge, whose proportions are only revealed as you walk away from it. Precipitous walls, honeycombed by mysterious caverns, enclose a succession of bays where shattered debris and inaccessible golden beaches are uncovered by the retiring tide. Several blowholes of massive proportions lie behind the cliff edge, their presence often concealed by the very flatness of the land. They will in time be invaded by the sea and add to the number of inaccessible bays that split the cliffs.

Above Saddle Point, the path turns in at Broad Haven, to the foot of Bosherston Lily Ponds.

BROAD HAVEN

Broad Haven, the first of two such named bays along the path, is a splendid sandy beach and became a fashionable bathing place in the nineteenth century. It is backed by sand dunes whose formation has been encouraged by the interruption of the water-flow from the valleys behind when the river was dammed by the Cawdors to form the Lily Ponds. The lakes occupy three sheltered river valleys that converge behind the beach. Their lime-rich waters and tree-lined hillsides provide a range of habitats that encourage a tremendous variety of both plants and wildlife. Together with the surrounding cliffs and land of the artillery ranges to the west, they are a valuable environment in which many rare species thrive. Indeed, it is one of the few places where I have watched otters play in the wild.

The coastline beyond Broad Haven lies within the Royal Armoured Corps Castlemartin Range, and access is subject to restrictions. You can often follow the coast from Broad Haven for some 7 kilometres (4.5 miles) to The Green Bridge. However, **there is no public access to the coastline between The Green Bridge and Furzenip**. The Coast Path diverts inland to follow the road through the village of Castlemartin before returning to the coast at Freshwater West.

Your onward choice of routes will be determined by operational activity on the Castlemartin Range (see Range Information). The cliff paths between Broad Haven and St Govan's Chapel, and St Govan's Chapel and The Green Bridge can be closed, and diversions through Bosherston and Merrion are then necessary. However, the paths are generally open at weekends. If you know that the range is closed the most convenient route lies through the Lily Ponds to Bosherston, described as an alternative.

Leave the Lily Ponds for the beach (signposted Coast Path), crossing the outflow stream by a wooden bridge on the right, and pass the dunes on their seaward perimeter. At the far end, a track

(signposted Coast Path) leads to a car park on the cliffs above. Continue on the cliffs beyond to a sentry post marking the eastern limit of the range.

Providing the range is open you can continue. A clear track follows a line well behind the cliffs to a car park at St Govan's Chapel. A less distinct path follows the perimeter of the cliff tops around Long Matthew Point, but you are reminded to exercise caution.

If the range is closed you must return to the car park and take the road to Bosherston.

Alternative: BROAD HAVEN to BOSHERSTON and CASTLEMARTIN

If the section beyond Broad Haven is closed it is convenient to go by the Lily Ponds to Bosherston. There are footpaths on either side of the western lake, both signed from where the ponds meet the beach. Either turn left and follow the lake's southern bank or continue ahead and then to the left over causeways which cross the bottom of the northern and the middle lakes. Continue up the western arm to the top. There, another causeway crosses the water to join the path along the southern bank. Continue ahead, climbing away from the lakes, to emerge by a National Trust car park behind Bosherston Church.

If the path between St Govan's and Green Bridge is open, return to the coast by turning turn left through the village, and walking along the road to St Govan's. If the path to Green Bridge is closed, you must now follow the road before the coast can be regained at Freshwater West. Turn right and follow the road out of the village to its junction with the B4319 at Sampson Cross, a little over 2 kilometres away. Turn left towards Castlemartin and continue past Merrion RAC camp to a crossroads, some 3.5 kilometres away. At this point, the lane from the left brings the Coast Path from The Green Bridge.

Savour the view from the cliffs before leaving Broad Haven. Star Rock lies below, and out to sea is the aptly named Church Rock. Beyond, there is a splendid retrospective view over Stackpole, whilst ahead the coast twists around a number of small inlets nestling under the grey cliffs of St Govan's. This prominence is the southern extremity of Pembroke and indeed of the Coast Path, and affords excellent views of the coast in both directions.

The scenery along the whole of this section is delightful. Blowholes, precipitous cliffs, caves and arches compete for your attention with the sea, which constantly swirls around outcrops of rock below. Tucked beneath the shelter of St Govan's Head is New Quay. As its name suggests, it was once used as a harbour; sheltered from the fury of storms its deep valley provided a relatively easy route to the high ground behind.

ST GOVAN'S

St Govan's Chapel lies near the bottom of a narrow gully in the cliffs, dropping steeply to a small rocky cove. The inevitable climb back is rewarded by the atmospheric setting of the chapel. Steep steps (the number of which, it is said, cannot be accurately counted), cut into the rock and worn smooth by the passage of innumerable feet take the path into the ravine, through the chapel and to the cove beyond. The tiny edifice is shadowed by towering cliffs and, below, countless boulders break the unceasing drive of the sea and starkly emphasise the isolation. Little imagination is necessary to visualise a hermit's lonely retreat, or the prayers of thanks that would have been offered at the simple altar for a safe landing on such a hostile coast.

Legend has never been hindered by a lack of fact, in this case the identity of St Govan. One story suggests Cofen, the wife of an ancient king of Glamorgan; another proposes Sir Gowain, one of King Arthur's knights. Popular theory, however, favours Gobham, a contemporary of St David and abbot of Dairninis in County Wexford, Ireland. Legend tells that in seeking refuge from pirates, he landed here and hid in a cleft that miraculously opened to conceal him until they had passed. He is said to have lived here until his death in 586.

The simple seaman's chapel is probably thirteenth century and consists of a single vaulted nave topped by a bell cote. A tiny spring inside the door was reputed to have curative properties. The altar is said to be the tomb of St Gobham, and behind is the fissure in which he is supposed to have hidden. The supposed rib marks in the rock are suggestive evidence, if not all that convincing. One thing is demonstrated: monastic life did not encourage obesity.

The cove below the chapel, bound between high cliffs, is wild and even on the brightest day remains desolate. Below the chapel, almost hidden amongst the boulders, is a tiny stone structure covering a spring. It also was attributed with healing properties and although now dry was visited by the afflicted until the middle of the last century.

St Gobham, in addition to the self-imposed hardships of his devotional life, also seems to have been unduly harassed by pirates. Another legend tells that raiders stole the church bell, which was made of silver. However, the boat foundered in a storm and the bell was returned by sea nymphs. They entombed it in a boulder and it is said that if the rock is struck the bell will sound. Whichever rock before you has the distinction of being "bell rock" remains a mystery, but nothing is lost by spending a few minutes in idle experiment.

The westerly route is again controlled by a sentry post. When the range is open, you can continue over the stile and along the coast to Elegug Stacks and the famous Green Bridge. A clear route provides easy walking across a level terrain.

Alternative:
ST GOVAN'S to BOSHERSTON and CASTLEMARTIN

When the range to the west is in use, you must follow the road behind the car park into Bosherston and follow the described alternative to Castlemartin.

RANGE EAST

*To the right of the marked path (**inland access is prohibited**), the heath stretches away, contributing little interest to the landscape. However, the intricacies along the coast are a more than sufficient preoccupation. Caves, blowholes, ravines and bays riddle the cliffs and the temptation to walk along the edges of the sheer cliff is great; if you do, take care, particularly when it is wet or windy.*

There are many notable features along this section of coast. Not far west of the control post, the path sweeps back to avoid Stennis Ford, a deep sheer sided cove widening out from its constricted link with the sea. Beyond is Huntsman's Leap, a narrower defile some 40 metres (130 feet) deep, its access to the sea being little more than a vertical gash in the cliff bridged by fallen rock. It is said that a mounted huntsman escaping from his creditors cleared the gap in a single leap. Later returning to appreciate his accomplishment, he died of fright. Bosherston and Saddle Heads are separated by The Devils Barn, an inlet backed by a series of interconnecting cauldron-

like blowholes, cascading into each other through a series of arches. Other complex blowholes to the west of Saddle Head will further distract your attention. The observation posts along the cliffs are used to control shipping in the danger area when the range is in use.

The Castle, an isolated prominence with a spectacular blowhole on its eastern side, was conveniently exploited as a fort by Iron Age settlers. Their contribution to its natural bastions can still be seen in the banks and ditches that run from the blowhole across the promontory. As you walk beyond, look back; a massive cave penetrates its base, connecting the blowhole to the sea on both sides. Rounding Mewsford Point, the truly impressive scenery of Bullslaughter Bay comes into view. A sandy beach lies enclosed by cliffs, spectacularly perforated by holes, arches and caves. The confusion is enhanced by severe folding running parallel to the coast, which can be seen in the cliffs dominating either end of the bay. Moody Nose, a sculpted outcrop of rock projecting into the sea to the west of Bullslaughter, has a splendid natural arch piercing its tip. This promontory is the site of another Iron Age fort, with a bank and ditch defending the isolated higher ground. Further west is Flimston Bay, where more dramatic folding and erosion will again delay your progress. The caves and rocks at the western end are particularly impressive. There is access to the beach and it is thought to have been used as a landing. On the western cliffs above the bay is a plaque to the memory of a young soldier, Trooper Graham Thomas, who fell to his death in 1990. It emphasises the dangers that these unforgiving cliffs can hold.

The last kilometres/miles have presented ever more dramatic sights, and the final few hundred metres/yards before the path turns its back on the coast are no exception. The mass to the west of Flimston Bay is yet another promontory that has been protected by ditch and bank to create a defensible Iron Age encampment. Go through the defensive line onto the point to inspect, with care, perhaps the most awesome blowhole encountered along this coast. Walking around its perimeter, it at first appears circumnavigable, but a narrow gash, blocked towards the top, will force you to return by the same route. The abyss, known as The Cauldron is open to the sea through a huge arch in its southern wall, and on the opposite side through narrow clefts to the beach. Birds swoop through its spectacular portals to seek perches on its precipitous walls or ride in the winds that are funnelled out through the top.

To the west, sheer cliffs enclose small bays, whose bases are strewn with rocks and stacks, fashioned into grotesque shapes by the relentless pounding of the waves. The Elegug Stacks rise majestically from the water, the smaller pointed stack standing 40 metres (130 feet) above the wave cut platform on which it rests. The other, more massive and with a crowning allotment of sea beet, sea cabbage and tree mallows, is little lower than the cliffs themselves at 45 metres (150 feet). In spring they provide nesting sites for thousands of guillemots. It is the Welsh name for the bird, heligog, that has given the stacks their name. Razorbills, fulmars, kittiwakes and shags amazingly also manage to find space on the narrow ledges.

Immediately to their west stands The Green Bridge, perhaps the best known formation on this coast. A wooden platform on the far side provides a good view, particularly in the evening sun. The platform is itself on top of an arch equally worthy of scrutiny; this is best seen from above The Green Bridge. The arches and stacks represent different stages in the process of erosion. Weaknesses in the cliffs are exploited to create a natural arch, which enlarges until it collapses, leaving an isolated stack. That in turn will eventually also disintegrate to join the heap of boulders and be finally ground to sand.

RANGE WEST

Beyond, the coast lies within Castlemartin Range West, to which there is no general public access. However, the National Park conduct a number of excellent guided walks from here to Furzenip throughout the year. Dates of the walks are published in their free annual newspaper *Coast to Coast*, and details are available at Information Centres in the area; advance booking is necessary.

Range West's geological features are equally as impressive as those encountered between Broad Haven and The Green Bridge. Below Mount Sion Down, two valleys converge at an inhospitable rocky cove in the surrounding slabs of limestone. High on its eastern slope is a deceptively cavernous blowhole, almost hidden from above by the curvature of the ground. Beyond, the rock's regular striation suggests that conditions during the carboniferous period were subject to cyclical change, and presents an ever changing pattern of beauty. At Pen-y-holt Down, an isolated stack provides a nesting site for guillemots. A broad promontory to the east of the strangely named Hobby Horse Bay is the site of an Iron Age camp, and its triple embankments remain an impressive monument to its makers. Behind, an arch emulates that of The Green Bridge. Close to the cliffs in Hobby Horse Bay is another massive stack, and in the headland immediately to the west, two arches penetrate a vast blowhole, presenting a spectacle rivalling that of The Cauldron at Flimston.

Beyond Linney Head the contours of the coast change, and the cliffs present a rounded shoulder to the sea, diminishing in height towards Bucks Pool. The limestone comes to an end and is replaced by an extensive dune system, which has become established in the wide valley that runs inland behind the bay. Hidden in the dunes is Frainslake, a marsh wetland that has formed as a result of the interruption of drainage patterns by the encroaching dunes.

THE CASTLEMARTIN RANGE

The Royal Armoured Corps Castlemartin Range occupies some 6,000 acres of coastal land between Broad Haven and Freshwater West. It was formerly part of the Cawdors' Stackpole estate and contained a number of livestock and arable farms. During the Second World War the area was requisitioned for military use, but then returned to agriculture in 1945. In 1948 the land was purchased by the Ministry of Defence and with the Korean War in 1951 was reopened as a firing range. It has operated as such since that date.

In 1961 a reciprocal agreement with the Federal German Army has allowed their tank battalions to use the range, and there is now a permanent German Army staff based at Merrion Camp working alongside their British counterparts. The German presence provides a significant benefit to the local economy and soldiers from the base have enthusiastically contributed to a number of local projects, notably the restoration of the chapels at Flimston and Warren.

Originally, the only public access to the coast was at Elegug Stacks and St Govan's Chapel. However, following the establishment of the National Park in 1952, there was increasing pressure for greater access. In the late 1960s it was decided that future training would not involve the use of explosive ammunition on Range East, the area between Broad Haven and Elegug Stacks. The coastal strip was then permanently cleared of unexploded shells and made safe. Consequently, when the range is not being used for training purposes there is public access along the cliffs. The Army, however, still needs to carry out a certain amount of training using explosive ammunition, and this is confined to Range West. The impracticality of clearing a safe path at the end of each firing session means that general public access cannot be given. However, by joining one of the regular National Park guided walks you can see the cliffs of Range West.

Contrary to popular belief, Army use of the area does not cause indiscriminate and widespread destruction of the environment. Tank and vehicle movements are restricted to constructed tracks, and firing is directed at specific targets. Consequently the impact of their activity is extremely localised and controlled. The remainder of the range has largely been allowed to develop naturally, and many areas have become important environmental sites. Some 25% of the area has been designated Sites of Special Scientific Interest. A number of factors have contributed to this importance. The area was taken out of farming use before the widespread use of chemical weedkillers and fertilisers. Thus native flowers and plants have been able to survive over significant areas, whereas modern intensive farming in the surrounding countryside has marginalised much of the natural vegetation. During the winter months sheep and cattle are brought down from the Mynydd Preseli to graze. This contributes to the local farming cycle and produces a twofold benefit to the land. Grazing livestock provide a natural fertiliser and help control the scrub and long grass species that would otherwise quickly take over the whole area. Consequently wild flowers have ideal conditions in which to flourish in abundance. The naturally managed grasslands and dune systems provide habitats for many species. Insects, butterflies, birds and small mammals all thrive, forming part of a natural food chain. The relative isolation and non-interference has allowed many rare and endangered species to established strong bases in the area.

The area is also rich in geological features, and there are extensive cave systems penetrating the bedrock. The continuous undisturbed layering of the limestone provides an important fossil record of earth's history. Man's early presence is well represented in the artifacts discovered in the cave systems. Many are now virtually inaccessible and provide evidence of how the topography of the area has changed with time. Later remains of settlements, promontory forts and burials provide valuable study areas for archaeologists. Old land use patterns have not been erased by modern farming techniques and provide evidence of early farming and social practices.

Such an extensive and varied natural resource is rare in this country, and the Army actively cooperates in helping to conserve the area for both study and future preservation. A voluntary body, the Range Recording and Advisory Group, has been formed to suggest how the often conflicting demands of use and conservation can be balanced in a way that minimises detrimental impact and is compatible with conservation objectives. Consequently, without a general exclusion because of military activity, controlled access may otherwise have to be considered to retain what has developed into an almost unique environment in our increasingly overcrowded and intensively used countryside.

Having taken your fill of The Green Bridge and the Stacks, and unless joining a guided walk, turn away from the coast and walk past the car park along the lane towards Warren.

Flimston Chapel and Farm lie to the left of the lane about 1 kilometre (0.6 mile) from the coast. The early history of the Chapel is uncertain, but suggests that it was at one time associated with Monkton Priory at Pembroke. It dates from the twelfth century but towards the eighteenth century it fell from use as a church. In 1784 permission was given for its use as a granary. In 1903 it was restored as a church by Colonel and Lady Lampton to the memory of their three sons, two of whom had been killed during the Boer War. Later restoration has been carried out by staff from Merrion Camp. Services are held in it during the summer.

The derelict farmhouse and buildings adjacent to the church are the remains of a medieval farmhouse complex. Consolidation work by the National Park is currently being undertaken.

From the crossroads with the B4319, the shortest way to Castlemartin is left into the village, some 2 kilometres (1.25 miles) away. That way may occasionally be closed but the alternative, although slightly longer, is perhaps a more pleasant walk. Cross over the B4319 and go ahead to the village of Warren whose church stands on top of the hill. At the top, turn left past the church and then fork left to leave Warren. At the end of that lane, again turn left to Castlemartin.

Warren church was, until recently, derelict and has been beautifully restored as a joint project between British and German soldiers from Merrion Camp. The spire, a prominent feature on the hillside, was apparently used as a navigation check by Luftwaffe navigators during the Second World War. Inside is an organ, built in 1842 and at one time belonging to Mendelssohn.

Both routes to Castlemartin converge at a small roundabout that was at one time a medieval pound in which straying cattle were confined; redemption to the owner was only after payment of a fine to the lord of the manor. It is now maintained as a public garden. The village can claim two notable

Natural arch to west of Green Bridge

Marloes Sands
Little Haven - Settlands

agricultural credits: a successful longhorn strain of cattle, known as Castlemartin Blacks, was improved from the native black cattle in the 1800s by the agricultural pioneer John Mirehouse of Brownslade, and at the beginning of that century, a certain Sir John Owen of Orielton received a Gold Medal from the Royal Society of Arts for his work in draining marshland in the area to create productive farmland.

Pass the cattle pound and follow the B4319 (signed Freshwater West and Angle) through the village. After some 3 kilometres (1.8 miles) the road drops to the coast at Freshwater West.

Above the beach to the left of the road is a small thatched hut restored by the National Park. It is the only remaining example in the area of a seaweed drying hut. An edible seaweed, Purple Laver, was once harvested here and used to make Laver Bread. The crop was washed and boiled for several hours to produce a gelatinous pulp. Old recipes recommended that it be fried with bacon and served for breakfast. It became a popular delicacy at the end of the last century, promoted by Alexis Soyer, the French chef of the Reform Club in London. A small industry grew to satisfy the demand. The seaweed was collected by villagers from Angle and dried on the floor of huts similar to this, before being sent by rail to Swansea for processing.

The car park behind the beach was the site of a Mesolithic settlement. These Stone Age people left few traces of their presence in this area, but archaeological excavation of the site some years ago produced a large number of worked flints.

Chapter Four

FRESHWATER WEST to PEMBROKE

31.2 kilometres (19.4 miles)

Beyond Freshwater West the landscape dramatically changes as the bedrock reverts from limestone to the underlying sandstone, although it does makes a fleeting reappearance in the bays of West Angle and Angle. Delightful, though occasionally strenuous walking leads onto the Angle peninsula, and then around into the sheltered estuary of Milford Haven.

Descend onto the beach opposite the car park, and turn north along the foot of the sand dunes towards low sandstone cliffs ahead. There, leave the beach, cross a stile at the edge of the dunes and follow a clear path that winds successively around East and West Pickard bays.

At first the path climbs easily as the cliffs gain height towards the west. Bracken and gorse blanket the sloping hillside, providing cover for rabbits. On the shallow point dividing the two bays, the path crosses through, and then for a short distance follows, the ditch and bank of a promontory fort. There is a splendid view along 3.5 kilometres (2 miles) of beach to Linney Head. In front, on the opposite side of The Haven, is St Ann's Head, and beyond the island of Skokholm.

The path gradually becomes more rugged, diverting to avoid some landslip above Whitedole Bay. After Castles Bay the path dips to cross a drainage valley and it then becomes easier as it rounds the most westerly point of the Angle peninsula. It is waymarked around the remains of the Victorian blockhouse.

Past Guttle Hole, a jagged arch through a protruding tongue of rock, is the remains of a curious hexagonal stone tower, variously described as a lighthouse or lookout tower. On the neck of land overlooking Sheep Island is another Iron Age fort and settlement, dated at around 300 BC; contemporary remains have also been found on the island. On the southern side of the valley just past Castles Bay, is a huge blowhole known as Welcome Pit; the best view is to be had from the opposite side as the path climbs away.

The point marks the entrance to Milford Haven and has been defended

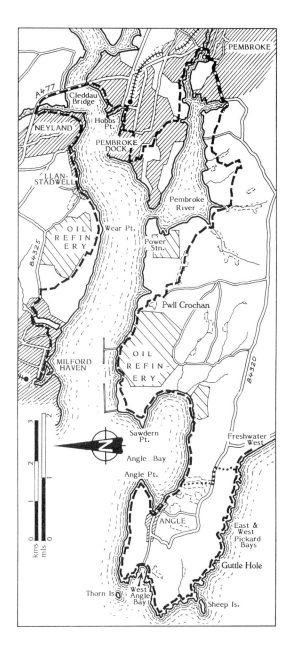

since prehistoric times. Rat Island, a misnomer since it is part of the headland, was settled by Iron Age people and oblong depressions in the ground have been identified as traces of their huts. The ruined tower is Elizabethan and was built in response to the threat of a Spanish invasion. More substantial fortifications were erected in the nineteenth century, when East Block House and its associated battery were built as part of the defences designed to protect The Haven and the Naval Dockyards at Pembroke. This fort, together with another on the Dale peninsula opposite, were intended to control access to The Haven. The fort has been demolished, but the impressive gun emplacements remain to the right of the waymarked path as it rounds the point. More recently there was an RAF radar station here, but its military use finally ceased in 1979.

Leave the point at the northern end along a gravel drive, and after passing a disused building, go left along the seaward edge of a field. The path drops through a copse of scrub and then winds along coastal field margins to a small café at West Angle Bay.

Ahead, the chimneys of the Pembroke oil refinery are a contrasting backdrop to the quiet village of Angle. It nestles in a shallow valley running back along the base of an anticline; the valley floor is limestone, flanked by sandstone slopes. Action of the sea on the low cliffs on either side of West Angle beach has left a complex of rocky coves and pools.

Once the site of a brickworks, a chimney by the café is all that remains. Now, the beach is popular with holidaymakers. Overlooking the sea from the car park behind the beach is a large bulbous cannon that has been resited from one of the batteries. A short distance away a plaque commemorates the Allied squadrons that operated from Angle Airfield during the Second World War.

Turning its back on the open sea, the route heads into The Haven estuary to seek a convenient crossing of this aquatic invasion of the land. The way is not taxing and encompasses as wide a variety of terrains and environments as any stretch of the route. Low cliffs and inclined slopes follow the edge of a sandstone ridge that parallels The Haven as far as Pembroke Dock and whose ruddy complexion will dominate the scenery ahead. Its form is not immediately obvious since it is broken successively by Angle Bay and the estuary of the Pembroke River. Beyond Angle Bay the course of the path avoids the industrial complexes, and eventually leaves the coastal strip to join the road into Pembroke.

MILFORD HAVEN

Angle is Norse meaning "turning" or "corner", and aptly describes the pivot about which The Haven turns, forced by the mass of St Ann's Head on its way to the open sea. The Welsh name Aberdaugleddau is equally descriptive: "the estuary of the two Cleddau rivers". The valley is a classic example of a ria or drowned river valley. It was cut when sea levels were lower, and further deepened by torrents of water released by melting ice some 20,000 years ago as the last Ice Age came to an end. That same melting caused a dramatic rise in sea levels, drowning its lower reaches to create the deep-water estuary we see today. The same effect can be seen at many other places, for example Solfach and Porth Clais.

The valley has been a focus for man since he first arrived in the area. In antiquity, water tended to be a link rather than a barrier, encouraging travel and communication. The winding waterway reaching far into the hinterland would have been readily utilised as an effective highway. The countless bays and streams lining its banks would have provided shelter from the open sea, and offered secluded havens from marauding bands of warriors. The development of agriculture and trade encouraged settlement around its shores, and as civilisation progressed, its advantage as a safe, deep-water harbour came to be fully appreciated. Its importance was already established when Norman invaders settled at Pembroke, founding what was to remain, until the coming of the railways, one of the major trading centres of the region. A focus for coastal and continental trade, it has remained an important link between Britain and Ireland. What was once one of Britain's largest fishing fleets grew up along its banks and a rich surrounding countryside encouraged productive agriculture.

In the sixteenth century the estuary was described by the Pembrokeshire antiquarian George Owen as a "large and spacious harbour...sufficient to receive the greatest vessel of whatsoever burden that saileth on the seas..". He went on to acknowledge its strategic importance by recommending that its mouth be fortified. Nelson, some 200 years later, proclaimed it as being second only to the harbour at Trincomalee, on the north-east coast of Ceylon (present day Sri Lanka). These attributes were realised during the second half of this century by the major oil companies. Sheltered deep water close to the shore allows massive ocean tankers direct access to the refineries and storage depots that have been built on the banks of its lower reaches.

Although a fine harbour, its approaches are complicated by reefs off the coast and in the entrance channel. Modern navigation towers help guide shipping along the narrow deep-water channel and dredging is necessary to provide sufficient clearance for the bigger ships that use it today.

Industry and habitation have exploited both banks of the estuary's middle reaches, but there is still much pleasure and interest to be derived along the 64 kilometres (40 miles) or so of path to St Ann's Head. The winding path creates another dimension for observation; the view to the opposite coast, for the most part less than 2 kilometres (1.25 miles) away, emphasises the inter-relationship of land and sea.

For much of the way the path maintains a detachment from the surrounding industrialisation, away from the hustle and bustle of daily life. Where possible it remains on the fringes of urbanisation, seeking secluded oases where the less obtrusive business of agriculture allows a more contemplative appreciation of the terrain. There remain a surprising number of spots which have either been ignored in the quest for development, or have since fallen from use to be reclaimed by nature's pervasive activity. In these refuges, nature retains its domination over the less sensitive activities of man. Open cliffs and foreshore contrast with richly wooded slopes and hollows, some of which hark back to the original native woodland that once clothed the area.

Milford Haven, stretching inland some 20 miles and having a tidal shore of around 110 miles, provides many important wildlife habitats. The seawater channel, influenced by the Gulf Stream combines with fresh waters from many rivers and streams to create a variety of conditions in which wildlife thrives. These are supported by intertidal flats, marshy shore lines and pockets of land that have been ignored by development. The encompassing agricultural activity allows some footholds for wildlife, as do, sometimes surprisingly, the towns and industrial sites which demand their own water frontage.

Although not visited by the path, many of the higher reaches of the Cleddaus are quiet and remote, and contain a number of important habitats. For those with time to spare they provide a diversion, rich in animal, plant and bird life. The rewards for a few additional days' wandering along their quiet banks are immense.

The waterway has been a focus for many events in Britain's history, and there is much of interest to see as the path follows the course of this elongated river-mouth. Changing fashions of defence and fortification are displayed, as too are some of the achievements of industrial and architectural ingenuity. The incorporation of aesthetic elegance with functionality in the ancient *castles and ecclesiastical buildings contrasts with the stark technological precision and complexity of modern industrial plant. A robust confidence in the permanency of new enterprise brought by the industrial revolution competes with the echoes of a less certain, but richly productive past.*

At the far end of West Angle car park a gravel track climbs above the cliffs north of the beach. In a short distance the track turns sharply right, but continue ahead along a path (signposted Coast Path) around the point and then up The Haven.

The headland gives a fine vantage of the lower reaches of The Haven. The channel is often busy with shipping, and recent years have seen the number of pleasure craft increase, encouraged by the development of marinas at Neyland and Milford. Thorn Island opposite West Angle, now a hotel, together with Stack Rock, isolated in the middle of the channel, were the two water based forts of The Haven's Napoleonic defences. On the opposite shore, a succession of lonely bays and low rocky cliffs sweep from the tip of Dale peninsula to Sandy Haven lying due north. Fields rise to the far skyline, and to the east, bare green terraces mark the now cleared site of Esso's oil refinery. Only its terminal jetty and umbilical pipeline remain to dominate the centre of the channel. Upstream, the adjacent Amoco jetty reaches out, as if to couple with that built from Popton by BP. In the distance, behind the buildings of Pembroke Dock, the Cleddau road bridge spans high above the river, dwarfing the insignificant specks of the boats below.

THE DEFENCE OF THE HAVEN

Formal defences date to Henry VIII when two blockhouses were built to guard the outer entrance to the channel; fragments of the eastern one still survive. Later wars and threats of invasion encouraged sporadic planning and even building. However, it took the establishment of a naval dockyard and the threat of French invasion for comprehensive plans to be drawn up at the beginning of the nineteenth century. Work on a fort had been started at Paterchurch, now Pembroke Dock, following the outbreak of the Seven Years War in 1756, but it was not completed. In 1817 a commission under Major General Bryce made proposals and, although nothing was done at the time, the subsequent defences were based on his strategy.

The unfinished Pater Fort was eventually completed in 1830, but was only garrisoned for a year. It was later dismantled in 1837 and replaced by a Battery in 1842, to protect the new naval dockyard. The immediate dockyard defences were further strengthened during the following decade by two "Martello" towers placed at either end of the dockyard and supported by a barracks on the high ground behind the docks.

Between 1850 and 1870 nine forts were built to provide outer defence along The Haven's banks. East and West Block Houses, Thorn Island and the fort at Dale guarded the entrance. Chapel Bay, Stack Rock and South Hook were designed to impede passage as the corner was turned, with two more forts at Popton and Hubberston providing further defence upstream. Fortifications on St Catherine's Island at Tenby and at Scoveston, on the high ground to the north of Hazelbeach, were also built at the same time. The threat of land attack was also considered and their design incorporated deep moats and high curtain walls.

The elaborate and costly defences were never tested, politics shifted, and the coming of a new century brought a different technology to warfare that rendered the defences largely irrelevant. Collectively they are referred to as Palmerston's Follies, a reference to the Prime Minister of the day who oversaw their construction. Although soundly conceived, they were built out of their time. A folly implies no purpose, and these buildings certainly can not be dismissed as such. They remain as much a visible demonstration of military strategy as the Norman castles of some 700 years earlier.

After 0.75 kilometre (0.5 mile) the path becomes bound by hedges and is forced inland around a copse of woodland.

On the left, almost hidden by trees and bushes, is Chapel Bay fort. Inquisitive adventurers should exercise caution, as its landward flank is protected by a deep and sheer moat. Although hidden by a creeping profusion of vegetation, it remains as effective today as it was when dug in 1870. The main entrance to the fort is at the south-east corner, but there is no access. Ahead to the right lies Angle. There has been a settlement here since early times, and the long narrow fields above the village date back to the Norman feudal strip farming system.

Beyond the fort, the path passes two cottages before crossing a stile (signposted Coast Path) into a thick wood covering the slopes above the waters.

In spring the trees provide a verdant canopy over a lush bank of bluebells and are a pleasant contrast to the open sea facing cliffs. As the woodland clears, the view ahead is dominated by a tangled complexity of pipes, tanks and chimneys, the Texaco refinery.

A succession of field boundary stiles leads to a gravel road above the new Angle lifeboat station. Cross to a stile opposite and

continue ahead around Angle Point. The field path ends at an unpaved road by a low white building, the Old Point House, a simple but attractive pub.

The lifeboat station was established in 1868 and originally known as the Milford rather than the Angle lifeboat; its designation was changed in 1892. The first station was a few metres/yards east of the present boat-house; its ruins can be reached through a gap in the hedge on the Point. Its replacement in 1927 stood alongside the present station, but was demolished in 1992 after the present boat-house was brought into service.

The station's roll of honour precedes its establishment with three silver medals being recorded for rescues carried out from the shore. The first was in 1833 to William Field who swam through surf to rescue twelve people from the brig Felicita. In 1851 Thomas Landells took a shore boat to rescue eight people from the schooner Maria. On another occasion John Large waded out "in peril of his life" to save three people from the wrecked brig Harmony.

Beyond the pub, the road follows the tidal limit around the inlet to a junction with Angle's main street in the village.

ANGLE

Angle's relative isolation has been instrumental in it remaining a quiet village, less affected by visitors than most. Enclosing arms of the bay separate it from the main stream of The Haven and shelter it from the wind. The oscillating tide gently washes a large expanse of mud flats and low beds of rock, replenishing a feeding ground for curlew, widgeon, dunlin, oystercatchers and many others, who strut about at low water, diligently probing the surface.

To the right, a single street follows the base of the valley, passing St Mary's Church, dating from the Norman era. Behind it is the later "Fisherman's" Chapel dedicated to St Anthony. Inside, above the doorway, is a plaque dedicated to its builder "Edward Shirburn of Nangle", and on the floor a recumbent stone effigy, its hands bound together in saintly prayer. To the north of the church, beyond the creek, stands a stone tower, all that remains of a castle. Tradition has it that three women became joint heiresses to the manor. Each built a castle, of which this is one. The remains of the second lie to the south-west of the church and the third is the present hall to the south-east overlooking the bay. The other notable architectural feature of the village is the Globe Hotel, further west along the main street. Its embattled upper storey overhanging the pavement and supported by six columns is an unusual contrast to the rustic cottages surrounding it.

Turn left and follow the road out of the village beside the shore; ignore the signposted road to Pembroke on the right. Continue past Angle Hall (the third castle) until the road turns right, away from the shore. There, a track leads to the beach; follow the shoreline around the head of the bay. Very high tides may cause inconvenience as there is no clear path along the field edges above the bay.

Dominating the skyline ahead is the Texaco refinery. Huge tanks and globular retorts are interwoven in a maze of connecting pipework from which tall chimneys emerge, dribbling white smoke into the breeze. Others vent banners of flame, like parodies of birthday cake candles. Behind the eastern corner of the bay, grassy terraces and service roads are all that remain of BP's oil storage depot. It was serviced by the oil terminal at Popton Point, and connected by pipeline to a refinery at Swansea. Signs of industry from an earlier era lie hidden in a copse of trees about half way along the beach, an old and ruinous limekiln.

Leave the beach at a convenient point by the former BP depot to join a service road running from its gatehouse around the eastern edge of the bay to Popton Point. Immediately before the fort, turn right (signposted Coast Path) and walk ahead, leaving the road beyond the fort across a concrete hard-standing to a stile (signposted Coast Path). A field path takes you onwards, dropping to the shore at Bullwell Bay and then again a short distance beyond to pass underneath the Texaco jetty.

Fort Popton was completed in 1864, but like its contemporaries, its strategic importance was short-lived. Used during the Second World War by the RAF, it then remained empty until 1961 when BP took it over as the headquarters for their pipeline terminal. It has since found a new lease of life as a research centre for the Field Studies Council. Overlooking Bullwell Bay, the large wooden object above the path is a transit marker to assist shipping passing along the channel.

MILFORD HAVEN AND THE OIL INDUSTRY

An exponential demand for oil after the Second World War stimulated development of ever larger tankers for transporting crude and its refined products around the world. The natural assets of a sheltered deep-water harbour, relatively close to the industrial centres of Wales and the English

Midlands, were soon realised by the oil industry. The boom years of the 1960s and early 1970s saw five separate companies establishing storage and refining installations around the fringes of The Haven. Esso was the first to arrive in 1960, building a refinery on the northern bank at South Hook Point. Its jetty, like those that came after, was built to the edge of the deep-water channel to provide berths for the massive tankers. Connecting pipelines link them to the shore, cradled high above the waters on concrete trestles.

BP arrived the following year with a terminal at Popton, feeding a row of storage tanks that stood on the rising ground behind the south-east corner of Angle Bay. The crude was piped to their refinery at Llandarcy some 100 kilometres (60 miles) away. Directly upstream in 1964, Regent Oil (now Texaco) constructed their refinery, which stretches inland to Rhoscrowther and dominates the hillside to the east of Angle Bay. Its jetty, together with that of BP, stretches for almost 2.25 kilometres (1.5 miles) along the coast. Gulf Oil appeared in 1968, opening their plant on the shores of the northern bank between Neyland and Milford. The most recent company to establish its presence is Amoco (now Elf) who operate a jetty, again on the northern bank, connected by pipeline to their refinery north-west of Milford. This refinery commenced operations in 1973. More recently, in 1977, a joint venture between Gulf and Texaco was commissioned. Known as the "cat cracker", it increases the proportion of "lighter" fuel products that can be refined from the crude base. It allows a more efficient use of resources in a changing market where there is less demand for heavy fuel oils. The plant is located on the Texaco site and connected to the Gulf refinery by pipeline. Much of the oil leaves as it came, by sea, but a significant amount is distributed throughout the country by pipeline. The Gulf and Elf plants have their own railway links, and a small proportion of products leave for more local destinations by road.

The changing fortunes of politics and economics has lessened the overall demand for oil, and the first companies to appear in The Haven have now departed. By the end of the 1980s the Esso and BP installations had closed. Industrial dereliction has been minimised by the removal of the storage tanks and pipework, leaving only grassy terraces and the terminal jetties into the channel.

Oil has had a significant impact in The Haven. It has provided employment, and also helped to generate supporting industries and an infrastructure that has benefited many local people. Although employing far fewer than during the peak of the mid 1980s, the oil companies remain a major economic factor. In no less a way have they impacted on the physical environment. The plants occupy large areas and operate processes which, if not contained, are potentially disastrous to the environment. But a responsible and positive attitude is developing that, whilst recognising economic need, acts to reduce pollution. Indeed research by The Haven companies has developed specialist techniques to deal with oil pollution which have been employed to meet emergencies elsewhere. Efforts are made to both minimise their impact and promote conservation. Gulf Oil in particular has a close association with the Wildlife Trust, and actively supports its conservation work. The sites cover large areas, much of which are undisturbed and provide habitats for many birds, mammals and insects. Whilst some might remain critical of the relationships between industry and nature, positive action to create an improving future is more effective than endless debate over past mistakes.

Beyond the pipeline, a path climbs the gorse covered hillside to a field, and continues up towards the refinery perimeter fence. A field track to the left roughly parallels the fence, periodic signs guiding you away from the coast to eventually arrive at a field gate. Beyond, a track drops to a bridge at the head of a marshy creek above Pwllcrochan Flats.

The full extent of the Texaco refinery is revealed to your right, the plant spreading back over the hillside. Ahead, in complete contrast, rising above the surrounding trees, is the pointed octagonal steeple and square tower of Pwllcrochan Church.

Across the bridge, the track becomes a pleasant wooded lane leading up to the few remaining houses of Pwllcrochan.

Once a thriving community, it has all but disappeared, as families have moved away from the shadow of the refinery. The church is secularised, although some of the graves that surround it are still tended. The village was a focal point for the surrounding farms, and Sunday morning service was as much a social as a religious event. It was apparently the custom at the turn of the century for a contingent of soldiers to march from the fort at Popton in full dress uniform to attend church parade. In earlier times the churchyard was the site of a skirmish, when a local militia group from Easington attacked some of Cromwell's troops. They were attempting to land stores in the creek below to support an attack on the castle at Pembroke.

Turn left by the church and follow the lane to a junction. Take the left fork (signposted Coast Path) and continue to a sharp left-

hand bend in the road. A path over a stile on the right crosses to a road on the far side of the field. Go through a small car park opposite and leave by a track at its far end, to pass around the southern perimeter of the Power Station.

Such a concentration of fuel production led to the construction of an oil powered electricity generating station. It was built on land reclaimed from a little creek, Pennar Gut, which ran down to the Pembroke River ahead. Being sited in a hollow, as is much of the Texaco refinery behind it, its visual impact is largely minimised, although little can be done about its towering chimney. It was designed to produce up to 2,000 megawatts of power, with space to expand if necessary. However, rising oil prices and lack of demand make it doubtful whether this will be realised.

Beyond a copse of woodland and a small stream that used to run into Pennar Gut, pass into a field. Go ahead to the top hedge and turn left along a track. It terminates at a field gate, beyond which field paths lead to Lambeeth Farm. Walk past the farm buildings and then go left where a stile at the rear of a wooden hut crosses to another hedged track.

There is little of spectacular interest along this section of path, but the way is pleasant through quiet farmland, copses of wood, old forgotten tracks and secluded valleys that carry a succession of streams to the muddy Pembroke River estuary. Although so close to industrialisation, nature's profusion is all around; waders, ducks and sea birds are busy on the mud flats below, hedges and trees attract a host of small birds, and the floor is carpeted with all manner of plants, which attract butterflies and other insects.

Often muddy, the track leads to and crosses a stream at the bottom of a wooded valley. After the inevitable climb, the path clears the trees and follows a field track to yet another hedged track, dropping to Goldborough Pill and meeting the stream by a large square limekiln. Follow the stream up the valley and over a stile onto a lane. Turn left (signposted Coast Path) and walk towards Hundleton. After about 1.3 kilometres (0.8 mile) turn left and go down a track to Brownslate Farm. Go through the gateway by the farmhouse, and immediately turn right to follow the wall to a copse of trees. A marked path over two streams leads up to a field stile beyond. Follow the left boundary to pick up a field track that eventually, after passing beneath power lines, rises to a gate onto a lane at West Grove.

To the left on the opposite side of the lane is a gated track (signposted Coast Path) leading to a field beyond. Keep to the right boundary to join a descending hedged path. At the bottom, take the right fork, cross a stream and field stile and continue ahead, eventually meeting a lane above Bentlass. Opposite, a track (signposted Coast Path) leads to a small sewage works, to the left of which is a field path. Continue onwards until eventually over a stile, the path joins a lane beside Fleet Cottage. Follow the lane left, to Quoits Mill (once the site of a watermill) and beyond to its junction with the B4320. Turn left and walk along the main road to Monkton Church. There, bear left into Church Terrace, known locally as "Awkward Hill", and walk down to meet the main road again at the bottom. Turn left to Monkton Bridge.

MONKTON PRIORY

Overlooking Pembroke Castle, Monkton Priory, a Benedictine foundation, was founded in 1098 on the site of an early Celtic Christian community. Its church served both the parish and the abbey, but after the dissolution fell into ruin. Remnants of the abbey's domestic buildings can be seen incorporated within the farm buildings at the side of the present church. The church, dedicated to St Nicholas and St John, was restored in the 1880s and embodies the choir and sanctuary of the original abbey church. Legend has it that a tunnel leads from the vicarage garden to the castle. Monkton Old Hall, part-way down "Awkward Hill", dates possibly to the fourteenth century, and is thought to have been associated with the monastery, possibly its guest house. The distinctive round chimney is characteristic of Norman construction in the area.

Monkton Bridge, below Pembroke Castle, used to boast a watermill and quay. The area upstream was formerly marshland which enhanced the castle's defensible position. The area is now drained, and its water level regulated by a sluice positioned downstream, which retains a picturesque pool around the castle.

Chapter Five

PEMBROKE to MILFORD HAVEN

20.4 kilometres (12.7 miles) see map p67

At Pembroke, or more particularly Pembroke Dock, we are at last able to cross the estuary. Before the modern bridge existed, numerous ferries carried people and cargo between the two halves of the county here. Once on the northern bank, we then turn, travelling downstream, to leave The Haven for the open sea once more.

We have so far remained on the fringe of industrial development, managing for the most part to avoid main roads. We are less fortunate for the next few kilometres/miles, as we pass through a succession of habitations: Pembroke, Pembroke Dock, Neyland, Milford Haven and Hakin. However do not despair, for in addition to allowing an opportunity to replenish supplies, eat a meal or call in at a pub without having to effect a substantial detour, there are relics of a rich historical past. In any case, the route does not lie entirely along built up streets, and where it does there are still points of interest along the way. There are surprises, even in the industrial heartland; rewarding views, pockets of greenery and odd corners where a feeling of remoteness returns.

PEMBROKE

Traces of early habitation have been found in the limestone caves of the area, but recorded history begins with the arrival of the Normans. Arnulph de Montgomery founded a castle in 1093 on the limestone promontory overlooking the Pembroke River. It was an ideal spot, protected by water on three sides and commanding a sheltered harbour at its foot. The settlement grew into a town along the ridge behind the castle. The fortification encouraged trade, and Pembroke rapidly dominated the area. An attempt to monopolise trade in the county was made in 1154 when the Act of Incorporation required all cargo passing into The Haven to be landed at Pembroke. Although the imposition was short-lived, the town retained its importance. The castle today is substantially that which existed at the beginning of the thirteenth century. It is an impressively complete building, dominated by high curtain walls and keep, and has figured in much of the town's history.

The prosperous and well fortified town not surprisingly attracted attention during the Civil War. Initially the Mayor, named Poyer, favoured the Parliamentary forces, but just before the war ended he switched allegiance to Charles I. Cromwell saw this as a rebellion that might escalate against him and attacked the castle in June 1648, leading the campaign in person. His siege lasted 48 days before the castle finally surrendered, and for Cromwell, just in time. By all accounts he was short of supplies, facing mutiny from his men and, to top it all, suffering from gout. He intended that the castle be dismantled to prevent further opposition and that the three leaders of the resistance be punished. They were sent to London for trial and condemned. However, it was decided to grant partial leniency by carrying out only one of the sentences. The decision was determined by lot, and Poyer was subsequently shot.

Cross Monkton Bridge and turn left to walk below the castle walls (signposted Castle Walk) to a car park on the old quay. (If you wish to visit the castle and town centre, instead continue up Westgate Hill. The castle entrance is towards the top of the hill on the left, and the town lies beyond.)

Ruins below the castle on the quayside are of warehouses and a customs house. On the bridge opposite was a watermill, still standing until 1955 when it was destroyed by fire. There used to be many grain mills around the coast, water providing the power to run them. Some were tidal, retaining water at high tide behind a barrage, others relied on the immediacy of a stream, although light summer rainfall could affect their working. Positioned along the coast they took advantage of the sea as an efficient means of transporting the flour to market, at a time when land travel was, to say the least, difficult.

Turn left at the main road, cross the bridge and walk up the hill. Part way up, turn left into Rocky Park (signposted Coast Path) and go to the end, where a tarmac drive leads to a field stile. Continue along field paths to a woodland track running above the river.

The castle stands impressively overlooking the river from its rocky promontory. The sluice gate below retains a pool around the castle, and controls tidal activity to help prevent flooding upstream. Depending on the state of the tide the Pembroke River can be a picturesque ribbon of water, winding its way from the castle, invariably with an odd boat tugging at its mooring. At low tide it dwindles to a trickle running between deep muddy banks, those same boats then wallowing in the mud, awaiting for the returning waters. Concealed in the thickets beside the path are the old quarries from which limestone was cut to build the castle and town.

Beyond the woodland the track again becomes a field path, which leads eventually to a copse of trees. Pass this on the left, cross a stream and squeeze-stile into the field beyond. Continue along the left boundary, finally leaving over a stile, the path then dropping through scrub to a farm track. Turn right and go up to a gate and stile which lead into the end of Sycamore Street.

There is now no alternative but to negotiate the paved streets of Pembroke Dock. There are any number of routes through the town, and preference will be governed by your eagerness to pass through as quickly as possible, or a wish to explore some of the town's history. The described route passes some of the sites that marked Pembroke Dock's development at the beginning of the nineteenth century, as it makes its way to the Cleddau Bridge, over which you must pass to gain the northern bank.

PEMBROKE DOCK

Pembroke Dock is a "new town", built to support the naval dockyard established at Paterchurch (Patrick's Church) in 1814. It was laid out with geometrical precision, and uniform buildings lined wide streets, criss-crossed in a regular grid. Prosperity derived almost entirely from military and civilian shipbuilding, with more than 250 ships and three royal yachts being constructed before the closure of the docks in 1926.

Activity revived during the Second World War when The Haven became an Atlantic base for both military and mercantile naval vessels. An RAF base for Sunderland and Catalina flying boats was also established. Unfortunately this concentration of military might attracted the unwelcome attentions of the Luftwaffe. A memorial clock at the entrance to the town's park in Bush Street remembers people who lost their lives during the heavy air raids which the town suffered.

The revival was, however, short-lived, and civilian enterprise has so far not replaced the economic benefits of past industry. Small industries have developed around the town, many with maritime associations, and B & I operate a ferry service to Ireland from the docks. The few remaining tugs moored offshore are now surrounded by a multitude of small pleasure boats, but the extravagant new marinas at Neyland and Milford Haven compete for the business of the leisure sailor.

Walk up Sycamore Street and continue along Hill Street; towards the top, take a path on the left across vacant ground to Treowen Road. There turn right, and then left into Cross Street. At the end a gap gives access to a footpath running along the eastern perimeter of a golf course on Barrack Hill. Turn right and walk alongside the barracks to the top of the hill.

The barracks hold a commanding position overlooking the docks to the north, and there is a fine view west along The Haven. The building was constructed in 1844 to accommodate the garrison manning the harbour defences. Its parade ground (the entrance is in the northern wall) remains an impressive example of nineteenth-century military architecture.

Turn left along the northern perimeter of the golf course to a small car park on the far side. Turn right onto the road and go down the hill. Part way down, where the road bends sharply right, turn left into a new housing development. Take the first right and then first left to emerge at a car park on the banks of The Haven at the end of Fort Road.

Off shore is a gun tower which, with the Pater battery to the north (demolished in 1903) and a second tower at the eastern end of the docks, formed the inner defence of the dockyard. They were completed in 1851 but improved artillery design quickly made them obsolete. Both towers were used as bases for anti-aircraft guns during the Second World War. Artifacts relating to Pembroke Dock's maritime past can be seen around the car park. The high wall alongside Fort Road encloses the old dockyard, where a number of elegant and imposing, if rather austere, buildings remain. The Irish Ferry and a number of businesses now operate from within the complex.

Leave the car park, heading east along Fort Road to the town. Turn left at the end into Pembroke Street, and go down to the waterfront.

Cargoes were landed from ships onto the quayside here at Front Street until the 1930s. The second of the two gun towers referred to at Fort Road stands at the bottom of the beach.

Walk to the end of Front Street and turn left, go past the supermarket to a roundabout. There, again turn left into Pier Road and walk to Hobbs Point at its end.

Hobbs Point once made an important contribution to both the military and economic life of the town. As a landing and embarkation point, it serviced the Llanion Army Barracks on the hillside to the east, and was the departure point for many soldiers leaving for the war in Crimea. During the town's industrial heyday, many of the warships launched from the dockyards downstream were brought here to be fitted out before commissioning. The quay was also used by passenger boats and subsequently a car ferry, linking the town with Neyland across the water. The opening of the Cleddau Bridge, 1 kilometre (0.6 mile) upstream, brought its operation to an end, and today only pleasure boats sail from the landing.

Retrace your steps along Pier Road until you reach a terrace of small industrial units on the left. Immediately beyond, turn left into an industrial estate. As the road bends right, take a footpath on the left to follow the line of the coast. It leads below the former Llanion Barracks (the large building to the right is now the Council Offices), a housing estate and the Cleddau Bridge Hotel, terminating at a road. Turn right to meet the main road and then left to cross the Cleddau Bridge.

The Cleddau Bridge is 820 metres (900 yards) long and carries the road 37 metres (120 feet) above the water on one of the longest single unsupported spans in Europe. It was built to replace the ferry service operating between Neyland and Hobbs Point, which had become unable to meet the increasing traffic demands of industrialisation and tourism. Work started in September 1968 and was finally completed in March 1975, having been interrupted by the tragic collapse of one of the sections in 1970, killing four of the workmen. The disaster questioned its box girder construction, and the project was redesigned before work commenced again in 1972. The final cost of around £12 million was four times that which had originally been anticipated.

Cross the Cleddau and continue over a second bridge above Westfield Pill. Immediately over the bridge turn left, where a path (signposted Coast Path) leads through a strip of woodland, high above the river, to Cambrian Road. Continue ahead to its junction with Picton Road. Turn left and walk down to Brunel Quay.

Alternative: WESTFIELD PILL to BRUNEL QUAY

Immediately over the second bridge, a track on the right drops steeply to the river. Turn right under the bridge and follow the river downstream past Neyland Marina to Brunel Quay.

Westfield Pill extends north for over 2 kilometres (1.25 miles) and was once tidal almost to its extremity. The construction of the marina necessitated the building of bunds upstream to prevent re-silting. This has created pools that now attract an impressive range of birds. Equally important as habitat for wildlife is the strip of ancient woodland that runs along its banks. It contains several rare plant species and attracts many insects, particularly butterflies. A walk upstream along the track following the line of the dismantled railway is a rewarding diversion.

NEYLAND

In 1856 Brunel established the town as the terminus of his Great Western Railway to link it with proposed Irish and Atlantic ferry services. Previously it had been a landing of little consequence, trade going to either Milford or Pembroke Docks, or passing on up the river. Brunel's original location for his terminus was Fishguard, but the idea was abandoned during the economic slump resulting from the Irish potato famine in 1846. He ignored the already established Milford Dock downstream and came here. A new town, dock, customs house and hotel were built around the rail terminus to service the international trade that was planned, and was given the name "New Milford". Traffic with Ireland brought success for a time, and attempts were made to establish an Atlantic trade. Unfortunately, being so far upstream, the waters were too shallow to accommodate the new passenger liners being built. The economic dream finally ended in 1906 when a deep water harbour and rail link were opened at Fishguard. The town, by then renamed Neyland, remained buoyant as a busy fishing port, with its own market and ice factory, and a ferry ran to Pembroke Dock and Hobbs Point.

1914 saw a decline in the fishing industry and the fleet moved to Milford Haven. Beeching's report in 1963 recommended the closure of the railway, the instrument which had first brought life to the town. Neyland was finally isolated as a backwater when the Cleddau Bridge opened and the ferry to Hobbs Point ceased to operate.

The quay area has been reconstructed to commemorate the vigorous, if short-lived prosperity that Brunel brought to the town. Memorabilia of its Great Age have been incorporated into its attractive landscaping. From here, the Cleddau Bridge dominates the river as it recedes from the busy industrial shores that border its lower banks. Upstream its fingers penetrate deep into the heart of the Pembrokeshire countryside, reaching inlets and creeks that at one time would have been busy with the trade of grain and other

Llanstadwell Church

commodities, but which today lie almost forgotten.

Opposite the entrance to Brunel Quay on Picton Road is an elegant Victorian letter box, removed from its original site on the former railway station. Its design is thought to have been conceived by the writer Anthony Trollope. The building next to it was formerly the station master's house.

Leave the quay along the service road to join Picton Road, turn left to The Promenade and continue along the waterfront.

Above The Promenade at its eastern end is Great Eastern Terrace, named in commemoration of the Great Eastern, Brunel's final and largest ship. It was built in Millwall in 1858, but twice visited the town for refitting. Directly across the water lies Pembroke Dock; the former naval dockyard lining the water-front is presided over by the barracks, high on the hill behind.

At the end of The Promenade turn left into Church Road (signposted Llanstadwell) and walk on to Hazelbeach.

At Llanstadwell the pretty church beside the road is dedicated to St Tudwell, a Welsh monk who died in Brittany in 564.

At the far end of Hazelbeach leave the road and turn left beside the Ferry Inn; the path leads to a grassy track, and after a few metres/ yards go left on a field path (signposted Coast Path) following the outer perimeter of the Gulf Oil refinery.

The refinery was opened in 1968 and has, with Texaco across the water, continued to invest in the area by cooperating in the building of the Cat Cracker" on the southern bank. The pipeline connecting the two plants is indicated by yellow diamond markers on both banks, and is crossed where the path briefly drops to the shore.

The path continues, bordered by security fences, crossing bridges over a service road to the terminal and then the jetty pipelines.

Both bridges are enclosed within a metal mesh, but the grided footways have been thoughtfully provided with a wooden walkway for dogs. The deep channel of the river comes close to the northern bank here, and you can sometimes see the tankers at close quarters as they discharge their cargoes through the waiting umbilicals. On the opposite bank the towering chimney of the power station rises out of the ground, a prominent landmark for miles around.

Beyond the second bridge the path emerges into a field; walk diagonally across it (signposted Coast Path) to a stile in the opposite corner. A grass track leads to a further stile, across which turn right

onto a gravel track, still beside the perimeter fence. Follow the track until advised by a warning that the route beyond is private property. A path on the left (signposted Coast Path) goes through the trees, across a stream and into a field. Go half right towards Venn Farm, skirt its buildings and emerge on a track at the entrance to the farm. Turn right and walk to the main road. There turn left and follow it to the bridge at Castle Pill. Take care as this section of road is narrow and traffic travels quickly around its bends.

Cross the bridge and, if the tide is out, take a path a few metres/yards beyond on the left down to the beach (signposted Coast Path). Walk downstream and join a track which continues along the high water mark.

Alternative: HIGH WATER

At high water continue along the road and take a track on the left that drops back towards the shore. A signed footpath leaves it on the right, just past an old limekiln, to emerge at Cellar Hill. There either turn right, and then at the top left, and walk down to the promenade; or alternatively turn left and try your luck again with the shore.

The track runs in front of a picturesque collection of cottages facing the water, overlooking a motley collection of working and pleasure boats. Depending on the state of the tide they will lie cocked askew as if asleep amongst the mud and stones, or lazily tug at their mooring ropes on the gentle swell of the tide.

Leave the shore with the track to climb Beach Hill. At the top, turn left along Murray Road and at the bottom, right onto The Rath, a promenade above sloping gardens. An alternative path parallels the road at the bottom of the gardens.

Towards the far end of The Rath is a bronze sculpture celebrating the town's past prosperity. A fisherman is portrayed gathering his nets, and below is an inscription "Thanks to them, Milford Haven flourished".

Beyond the statue turn left through the gardens and at the bottom follow a drive leading to the water-front. Just before the bottom go through a gap in the right-hand wall towards Milford Dock.

Chapter Six

MILFORD HAVEN to DALE
16.4 kilometres (10.2 miles)

MILFORD HAVEN

Before the nineteenth century Milford Haven was merely a collection of fishing cottages. The land was acquired by marriage at the end of the previous century by Sir William Hamilton, who through an Act of Parliament obtained permission to build a new town and dockyard. The work was undertaken by his nephew Charles Greville who persuaded a group of Quaker whalers, forced out of Nantucket by religious prejudice, to settle in his new town. They laid the foundations of success by producing whale oil, then in great demand as the main fuel for providing lighting. Fortune was short-lived, however, as the manufacture and use of coal gas was developed, thus obviating the need for oil.

Other possibilities were recognised by Lord Nelson, who had been encouraged to visit in 1802 by Lady Emma Hamilton, now Sir William's young second wife. He praised the natural features of The Haven, and promoted the building of a dockyard. However, the idea did not materialise, for although the Navy already leased shipyards from the family, Greville's heir demanded too high a price for the lease's renewal and in 1814 the Navy took their business upstream to Paterchurch and built Pembroke Dock.

Prosperity remained elusive until in 1888 a dock and harbour was finally completed. A busy fishing fleet developed, supported by the railway that had by now reached the town, and could send fish directly and quickly to inland markets. The town's other ambition, to attract Irish and Atlantic trade, was never realised, being lost successively to competition from Neyland, Fishguard and finally Liverpool.

The decline in fishing has had its effect on the town, although some advantage was gained in the heyday of the developing oil industry. Undaunted, a new future is being courted, and the development of a marina and leisure activities around the docks may well hold the key. The dock still supports a fishing industry and new packing and distribution facilities have been constructed on the western side.

The harbour remains a busy place, and worth investigation. Hard

worked fishing boats lie, some almost derelict, as a testament to the arduous and dangerous conditions faced in bringing home the harvest of the sea. Alongside, sleek and polished yachts, almost clinically clean in their perfection, depict another breed of mariner who joists with the dangers of the sea to relieve the monotony of "civilised existence".

The harbour contains several relics of the town's maritime past. Moored alongside the south-eastern wall is the restored Haven Lightship, and next to it, currently undergoing restoration, is a wooden gaff-rigged schooner, the Pascual Flores. At the head of the docks a number of railway engines which worked in the nearby refineries are displayed and there is a museum.

Beyond Milford Haven there only remains Hakin and the former Esso refinery to be passed before an uncluttered coastline is regained. Gentle ruddy sandstone cliffs, gradually increasing in height, twist and turn around a succession of tiny bays as the path works its way back towards the open sea.

In planning the walk to Dale it is necessary to bear in mind that two streams have to be forded, the first at Sandy Haven (SM 855 075) and the second at Pickleridge (SM 813 070). Both crossings lie within the tidal range of the estuaries that they occupy, and although looking totally insignificant on the map are sufficiently flooded by the incoming tide to make them impassable. Both can only be safely crossed within two hours either side of low tide. Careful timing of your arrival at the first, Sandy Haven, is necessary to allow you sufficient time (up to two hours) to walk the intervening 8 kilometres (5 miles) or so of coast to Pickleridge before

Lightship in Milford Haven Dock

that crossing becomes impassable. Those planning a day walk and requiring to make a return journey will, of course, need to be doubly vigilant. If you miss either, there is no readily suitable alternative crossing, and in both cases either a wait or substantial detour is necessary to reach the other side. Directions for the detours are given in the text.

The lock gates at the entrance to the dock are usually closed (which means they are open to pedestrians) except for some three hours before high tide. If this is the case, you can walk along the sea wall and cross the harbour entrance over the lock gates before walking up to the King's Arms.

If the gates are open (closed to pedestrians) walk around the landward perimeter of the harbour, leaving along a narrow road by the fish market on the opposite side. Follow the road past the marine repair area to the King's Arms.

Immediately beyond the Kings Arms, take a path on the left along the sea front. This eventually turns inland to join St Ann's Road. Go on to its end and turn left into Picton Road, following that until it bends sharply to the right in front of a school.

The departure from the coast is to avoid the premises of the Milford Haven Conservancy Board and Fort Hubberston. Turning left immediately before the school takes you to the fort. It is now derelict, suffering the effects of both nature and the more wilful attentions of vandals. Despite this it remains an impressive sight, and a short excursion to explore the barracks and gun battery below is justified. Take care as the buildings are littered with masonry rubble, hidden holes conceal underground rooms and there is a deep drop from the overgrown battery to the magazines below.

After visiting the fort, from its entrance, take a path on the left that drops to the coast road below. Alternatively, from the school, a path just beyond it on the left also leads to the coast road.

Follow the road around Gelliswick Bay, continuing ahead at its far end. Ignore the entrance to the Elf Jetty and carry on (signposted Coast Path) below some large houses. Beyond, follow the perimeter of the now dismantled Esso refinery. The path drops to the beach to pass underneath the pipework of its still standing jetty and then regains the rolling cliffs to pass around South Hook Point.

South Hook fort stands behind the boundary of the Esso site and was used by the company as a store. The gun batteries and their underground

Fort Hubberston

magazines lie closer to the path. The tanks of the refinery have now gone, but their foundation platforms and interconnecting roadways remain. In time nature may soften the still harsh contours, although at the moment it stands as a bleak reminder of the scale of man's industrial activity.

At South Hook the path heads north to Sandy Haven, leaving behind the industrialisation and urbanisation of the middle reaches of The Haven. There, it leaves the cliffs through a small caravan site onto a narrow lane. Continue ahead, past Ferry Cottage and down a slipway to the estuary.

SANDY HAVEN

Sandy Haven is a truly idyllic spot, its pleasure heightened by the contrast to the towns left behind. The banks are heavily clad in trees that reach to the water's edge, providing a lush background to the firm sands of the creek. The stream reaches back into a rolling landscape, suggesting secrets and mystery.

The most evocative and eloquent description I have read of this wonderful spot was penned by Graham Sutherland, responsible for among other things the tapestry Christ in Glory *commissioned for the cathedral at Coventry, in a letter to his friend and patron Colin Anderson, who had asked about the places that influenced his work. Sutherland first visited Pembrokeshire in 1934 but was repeatedly drawn back throughout his life and although he never painted in Wales was deeply influenced by its landscapes, extensively sketching what he saw. Not everybody might appreciate him as an artist, but I commend you to his letter, published in* Graham Sutherland *by Ronald Alley. The Sutherland Gallery is at Picton, to the east of Haverfordwest.*

Either luck or planning has hopefully got you here at the right state of the tide. If it is out, walk across the sand. The stream lies towards the far side of the estuary, and a number of well placed stepping stones allow you to get across without getting your feet too wet. Leave the beach by a slipway on the far side to join the St Ishmael's road. A short distance beyond the houses, take a path over a stile into the wooded bank on the left (signposted Coast Path).

Alternative: HIGH WATER 6.3 kilometres (3.9 miles)

The alternative is more protracted. Having wandered down the slipway to survey the waters and check that I have not been mistaken about being unable to get across, retrace your steps past Ferry Cottage. The name is significant as at one time a passenger ferry operated between the two shores, and would have saved you the long tramp. Unfortunately virtually all of the walk is on the road. Follow the lane towards Herbrandston. After 1.1 kilometres (0.7 mile), it bends half right. Take a signed footpath over a stile on the left. Cross the field to emerge in the village beside St Mary's Church Hall. There, turn left and walk through the village to join the main road. Continue over Rickstone Bridge towards St Ishmael's. Eventually a road on the left (signposted Sandy Haven) leads downhill past Sandy Haven Farm. At the end of the lane turn left towards the beach; the coast path leaves the road on the right.

Before taking the path, walk a few metres/yards further on where there is a well preserved limekiln and weighbridge. Behind, higher up the bank, the ruined workman's cottage lies hidden in the trees.

Emerge from the trees to a field and follow its left boundary to the corner. There, the path goes back into woodland above the creek and heads downstream to its mouth. It then continues on the edge of cultivation along the coast passing Little and Great Castle Heads to reach Watch House Point.

Both Castle Heads were chosen as sites for forts by Iron Age people; mounds were constructed across the base of the promontory in each case to create a defensible position. The mound and ditch at Little Castle is clearly visible. At Great Castle the path follows the line of the earthwork defence, cutting off the promontory. Two lighthouses, still shown on the map, have long since gone; their function has been replaced by navigation beacons and transit towers. The rectangular marker just passed, together with the triangular one at Bullwell Bay, are two of the transit towers. The remaining Haven markers will be passed on the Dale peninsula.

The scenery below is fascinating. Impressive but small bays succeed each other, the path in places close to the edge of massive slabs of sandstone rising out of the waters. The field banks beside the path are a mass of flowers in spring. At Lindsway Bay there is safe, albeit steep access to the beach below.

Watch House Point, looking directly at the open sea through the jaws of The Haven, was chosen for an artillery battery during the First World War. On the hillsides around the Point, now much overgrown and partly hidden by gorse and bramble, are the substantial remains of the open fronted gun shelters.

Beyond Watch House Point the path steadily loses height towards Monk Haven, where it drops into a richly verdant valley, running inland to St Ishmael's.

An impressive little tower stands sentinel over Monk Haven, and although possessing a Norman arch and lancet windows it is in fact a Victorian folly. The high wall across the beach is eighteenth century and was part of an estate boundary wall.

Hidden by trees, well sheltered and yet easily accessible to the sea, this spot has been a landing from earliest times. An ancient track connected it to the St David's peninsula, and during the Age of Saints pilgrims will have given thanks for a safe landing at the little church dedicated to St Ishmael just up the valley, before continuing their journey on foot to the cathedral city.

Cross Monk Haven, either to the left along the beach or alternatively by following the stream up the valley, where it can be crossed along a dam below a small pond. The onward path leaves the western end of the beach, climbing through woodland to the cliff tops and on to Musselwick Point.

Once above the trees there are splendid views across to Dale, nestling in the gentle cleavage of a shallow valley. To the left, on Dale Point, is another of Palmerston's forts.

From Musselwick Point the path loses height, and a succession of stiles and field paths leads to a farmyard. Pass the barns and turn left (signposted Coast Path) to drop beside a stream to the beach. Turn right and follow the beach round to The Gann.

Again, hopefully your timing has been impeccable and you can ford the stream which drains the marshy area to the north. The crossing is by a short causeway between the high shingle banks on either side. On the opposite bank a clear track across the top of the shingle leads to a small car park and the road. Otherwise you must either wait for the waters to subside or take the inland route.

Alternative: HIGH WATER 4.7 kilometres (2.9 miles)

Climb off the shore and go through a field gate back to the right (signposted High Tide Alternative). Follow the left field boundary up the hill. At the top, cross a stile on the left, again signed, and follow the right boundary to the buildings of Slatehill Farm. From there a track continues ahead across the fields to a narrow lane at Whiteholme's Farm. (The slightly shorter track from The Gann alongside the Saltings arrives at the same place, but is not a designated right of way.) Cross over the lane to a signed, although non too obvious track still heading north. It is initially overgrown but shortly emerges into a field. Go ahead along field paths, dropping to cross a stream before climbing to the road at South Mullock. Turn left (signposted High Tide Alternative) to Mullock Bridge. A further 1.5 kilometres (1 mile) of road walking leads to the car park at Pickleridge.

The topography at Pickleridge is the result of both natural and human activity. At the end of the last Ice Age meltwater deposits of sand and gravel choked the valley, leaving a marsh. During the Second World War, gravel was excavated for the construction of military airfields at Dale, leaving substantial pits. The sea has since flooded in and is slowly refilling them with stone as the coastline is gradually pushed inland.

This manipulation of the landscape has produced an environment attractive to wildlife. A large number of birds come to feed in the marshes and take advantage of the sheltered water. Winter is a particularly good time for birdwatching, with many species of ducks, geese and waders being recorded.

Turn left onto the road and follow it into Dale.

Chapter Seven

DALE to ST BRIDE'S

24.3 kilometres (15.1 miles)

DALE

The tiny settlement of Dale nestles in a shallow depression binding the peninsula beyond to the mass of Pembroke. In fact its very name is Norse for valley. The few buildings behind the stony beach look along the full length of The Haven to Pembroke Dock, their clear line of sight interrupted only by Stack Rock and the projecting fingers of the oil terminal jetties reaching out from opposite banks, as if to touch each other. Dale's present appearance belies its former importance when, during the sixteenth century, it served the surrounding area as a fishing and trading port. Industry has now given way to leisure and its reputation as the sunniest spot in Wales no doubt helps attract windsurfers and yachtsmen, who come to enjoy the sheltered waters of Dale Roads.

It was in a small bay nearby that in 1485, after 14 years in exile, Henry Tudor made an unopposed landing with a small band of supporters from the French port of Harfleur. Fifteen days later at the Battle of Bosworth he defeated Richard III to become Henry VII, King of England and founder of a dynasty that would last until the death of Elizabeth I in 1603. There is a commemorative plaque recording his landing in the village.

The path to St Ann's Head is a delightful walk, despite its first 1.5 kilometres (0.9 mile) following a metalled road. The projecting mass of the peninsula shelters the eastern coastline from the wind, and lush woodland fringes the coast and fills the hollows that have been left untouched by the plough. It is a chance to reflect upon the different environments which The Haven offered, and take a last look to the Angle Peninsula before emerging once more alongside the open sea. Beyond, the section between St Ann's Head and the Marloes peninsula is very much a contrast. Red Sandstone to the south and earlier Silurian shales to the north face the prevailing weather and present a rugged and exposed coastline. Vegetation is hardy and battered low by the salt laden air. However, past Wooltack Point the coast is

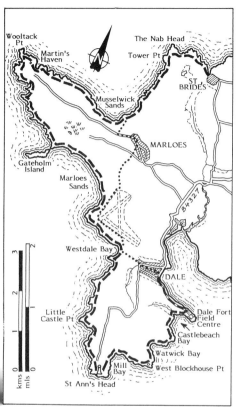

sheltered, and once again takes on a more gentle aspect towards St Bride's. The walking for the most part is relatively easy, the path maintaining its height, and making only infrequent dips that require re-ascent.

Remain on the coast road, keeping to the left as it climbs from the village towards Dale Fort. Shortly before reaching the fort, a path on the right (signposted Coast Path) crosses the peninsula, rejoining the coast above Castlebeach Bay.

Dale Fort has been used by the Field Studies Council since 1947. Its outer defensive wall parallels that of its earlier prehistoric counterpart, and it is interesting to note that the strategy of ditch and bank has survived almost unchanged through some 2,000 years of military defensive architecture.

Beyond, the path curves around Castlebeach and Watwick Bays, dropping at the head of each before climbing again to West Blockhouse Point, where it passes the last fort of The Haven's defences.

Watwick Point is dominated by a 50 metres (160 feet) high navigation beacon. There are more markers at West Blockhouse Point beside the small but interesting fort. It was built just after that on Dale Point and is now let as holiday accommodation. Gun emplacements and their associated bunkers, which were brought back into service during the last two wars, lie beyond to the right of the path.

Ahead, the path crosses grass slopes and then drops to the beach at Mill Bay, where Henry made his landfall. It then rises again towards St Ann's Head.

This stretch of coast offers a fine view across the mouth of The Haven. The changing perspective of the opposite coastline gradually reveals the distant shore of Freshwater West, culminating in the unmistakable vertical cliffs of Linney Head. In the middle distance Sheep Island gradually asserts its separateness from the backdrop of cliffs.

Climbing onto St Ann's Head, keep to the landward side of the walled garden, to follow a grass track towards a terrace of cottages by the lighthouse. Immediately before the cottages a fenceline forces the path right, passing through a gate onto a service road coming from the north. There is no public access to the cliffs around the point.

ST ANN'S HEAD

Always a prominent landmark for mariners, the headland was once the site of a chapel, said to have been built by Henry in gratitude for his safe landfall in the bay below. It has long since gone. Navigation into The Haven is complicated by submerged reefs and rocky outcrops off the coast. The first official beacon here in the middle of the seventeenth century was powered by coal. However the owners, who were only permitted to collect voluntary payments from passing shipping, became over-zealous and exceeded their licence. The light was consequently closed, and despite petitions for its re-establishment it was not until 1714 that two lighthouses were built. The rear light is now operated as a coastguard station and the other, re-sited further from the cliff edge in 1841 because of erosion, still provides a mark for shipping. St Ann's is the base control for all the lighthouses along the Pembrokeshire coast, and the adjacent helicopter pad is used by the servicing crew. The relative isolation of even a shore-based lighthouse is emphasised by the community of houses and walled allotment that cluster around the lighthouse. The nineteenth century jetty lying below the eastern cliffs was constructed to facilitate the safe landing of building materials for the station.

Cobbler's Hole at St Ann's Head

Before leaving St Ann's, walk along a fenced path at the side of the helicopter landing pad to view the cliff formation known as Cobbler's Hole. Erosion of the cliffs has exposed a magnificent example of the severe folding and faulting which has tortured the rock. The spectacular plication of the layers is reminiscent of a frozen tsunami in a Japanese painting.

Leave by the service road, and outside the boundary gate, turn left over a stile (signposted Coast Path) to follow an easy path along the cliffs to Great Castle Head and thence to Westdale Bay.

The gentle rise of the fields to the right contrasts sharply with the shattered debris below the cliffs. The boulders and detached outcrops of rock are constantly battered by waves venting their energy. Building rubble, visible in the field embankments to the right of the path, is from HMS Harrier, a radar and meteorological school which, before it closed in 1960, occupied a site on the cliffs. The National Trust now owns the land and has returned it to its former agricultural use.

Great Castle, a prominent headland overlooking Westdale beach, is aptly named. An impressive Iron Age fort occupies the promontory, and its intricate landward defences are readily discernible. From its height, the geography of Dale is more easily appreciated. The valley lies along the Rhydeg Fault, an extensive feature which runs the length of The Haven, continues along the Rhydeg Valley west of Tenby and is again evident on the other side of Carmarthen Bay, cutting across the Gower peninsula. The valley base slopes gently to the east, and is composed of glacial debris, evident in the low cliffs above Westdale, filling the gap separating the Dale promontory from the mainland. In geological terms the land connection is only temporary, and erosion will once more separate the peninsula as an island. The process appears as if it is being hastened by the work of trogloditic rabbits, each one of whom has a sea view at the end of its burrow. However the present panorama of the village, clustered behind the beach and overlooked by its church and artistically crenellated castle, will no doubt continue to delight both walkers and its inhabitants for many generations to come.

Having climbed out of Westdale, the path dips to cross a stream at Hook Vale before continuing more easily above Marloes Sands.

The concrete aprons occasionally visible to the right of the path remain from the wartime Dale Airfield. Ahead, rugged red cliffs curve to the north-west, leading the eye out to the large mass of Skomer in the distance. Out to sea is the smaller Skokholm, and tucked below the cliffs in the near distance, barely distinguishable as a separate entity, is Gateholm. Their names invoke memories of the Norse sailors who gave these islands their names. Holmen, surviving as -holm, means small island, whilst øy describes a larger island as in Caldey, Ramsey and Skalmey, the old name for Skolmer which describes its cloven shape.

THE ISLANDS

It is convenient to discuss the scattered islands off the coast as a group. An outcrop of resistant rock, geologically unique and known as the Skomer Volcanic series, runs from near St Ishmael's to the north-east of Dale, west along the Marloes peninsula and then out under the sea. It reveals itself in the geology of the Deer Park headland and the Skomer group of islands before emerging again at Grassholm and the further outlying tidal reefs known as the Hats and Barrels. It finally culminates at The Smalls, two bare projecting rocks 25 kilometres (16 miles) offshore to the west. The islands of Skokholm and Gateholm are of different formation, and their contrasting red cliffs betray their association with the younger rocks of Old Red Sandstone underlying St Ann's Head.

The Smalls and the nearer tidal reefs have always been a hazard to shipping, and in 1775 a Liverpool dockmaster John Phillips, following a personal disastrous encounter with them, erected a light on The Smalls. The initial construction was designed by a musical instrument-maker from Liverpool, a hut supported on wooden pillars that allowed the sea to wash beneath. It established a principle of sound design, still adopted in offshore drilling rigs, and the light functioned until replaced with a stone tower by Trinity House in 1861. This lighthouse still operates today, although now as an automatic light. It was of inestimable value to shipping and by the middle of the nineteenth century it had become the most profitable lighthouse in the world, collecting dues from British and foreign shipping using Irish Sea ports at the rate of 1d or 2d per ton of cargo respectively. Good binoculars can pick out the lighthouse on a clear day.

Grassholm, 12 kilometres (7 miles) west of Skokholm, is owned by the RSPB, and has never been permanently inhabited. Since the 1860s it has provided a home for an ever increasing population of gannets, thought to have originated from a colony on Lundy. Surprisingly, because of their huge numbers, the birds can be seen from the mainland through binoculars as a white patch on the island's cliffs. The cloud above is composed of flying birds, and gives the appearance of a smouldering volcano. Visitor access to the island is limited to minimise disturbance of the nesting birds.

All the other islands bear traces of past habitation. Skomer, the largest in the group and owned by the Nature Conservancy Council, bears extensive evidence of Iron Age settlement and was farmed from the eighteenth century. Since 1959 it has been managed as a National Nature Reserve, and is a breeding sanctuary for over 30 species of seabirds, the most numerous colony being that of Manx Shearwaters, whose nest burrows cover the island. Day visits can be made during the season which allow a first hand appreciation of the competition which takes place for nesting sites.

Skokholm was managed as a rabbit warren by the Normans, who first introduced the animal to the island. Their descendants (the rabbits' that is) compete with storm petrels for suitable nest burrows below its windswept surface. The island was farmed from the middle of the eighteenth century until 1939, when Britain's first bird observatory was founded there. Although privately owned, the island is leased to the West Wales Naturalists' Trust and managed as a reserve. Access is restricted to WWNT members and generally limited to weekly residential visits.

Gateholm, barely separate from the land and only an island at high tide, is geologically distinct from the landward cliffs a few metres/yards away, and of the same rock formation as Skokholm and St Ann's Head. It too bears traces of early habitation, including what is thought to be the remains of an early Christian monastic community.

During the summer, if you have the time, a visit where possible to the islands or a boat trip to explore their sea-washed cliffs is a rewarding experience. Boats leave from Dale and the small beach at Martin's Haven at the north-east corner of the Deer Park.

Beyond Hooper's Point, the underlying rock changes abruptly and visibly, from Old Red Sandstone to the earlier deposits of the Silurian period. Weathering of the near vertical beds has produced interesting formations; notable are the Three Chimneys, which rise in the cliffs about a third of the way along Marloes beach. Exploitation of softer rocks within the multi-layered sandwich has created three protruding ribs in the cliffs. Until 1954 they were augmented by a fourth "chimney", which was destroyed by an exceptional gale, demonstrating the impermanent nature of the cliffs. They are best appreciated from the beach below.

Above the beach the cliffs edges are friable, but the path is stable and is an easy and enjoyable walk. Towards the far end it drops steeply into a valley (where there is access onto the beach) and then climbs, eventually arriving at Horse Neck, a rocky outcrop delimiting the western end of the beach and overlooking Gateholm.

There is a steep path to the beach from here, and at low tide it is possible to cross the boulder strewn gap separating Gateholm from the landmass. Steeply sloping slabs on the north-eastern corner of the island offer a way up to its grassy plateau, where traces of ancient huts can be seen. The way is steep and care is needed, as is an awareness of the tide, if you wish to avoid being stranded.

The path on towards the tip of the Marloes peninsula offers more or less level walking above a now rocky shore, which replaces the fine sandy beach behind you.

To the west of Horse Neck, at low tide a crooked finger of ironwork projects from the sea, pointing vaguely onwards. It is all that is now visible of the Albion, a paddle steamer, which fell foul of the rocks on its maiden voyage to the Bristol Channel around 1840.

A short distance on, beyond a small stream, the path rises to meet and follow the embankments of a prehistoric settlement.

The fortifications remain impressive and enclose a small amphitheatre commanding an excellent view along the cliffs. The rocks below are spectacular, outcropping slabs presenting abrupt faces to meet the force of the driving sea.

Walk ahead to the Deer Park, which is contained by a wall following the line of a meltwater valley across the neck of land to Martin's Haven on the northern coast of the peninsula.

DEER PARK

The peninsula, once part of the Kensington estate whose seat lay to the north-east, was enclosed at the beginning of the nineteenth century. The title Deer Park is perhaps a pretentious misnomer as there is no record that such animals were ever kept here. The wall parallels a fortification a little further to the west, which protected an Iron Age settlement on the promontory. The coast path is here signed to the right, following the line of the wall, but it is worth a short detour to explore the headland and enjoy the view across the intervening sound past Midland Isle to Skomer.

Cross the wall and take a path along the cliffs. Towards the far corner the route is diverted inland along a marked track in order to protect an area adopted as a feeding ground by choughs, who now breed on the point. The path shortly returns to the cliffs above the sound and continues to Wooltack Point. After savouring the impressive scenery, here of volcanic rather than sedimentary origin, turn east and climb to a small white building occupying the high spot of the Park.

Once a coastguard lookout, it now houses a small display describing

Cliffs to the east of Renney Slip, Deer Park

some of the features of the area, and the way in which the landscape is being managed to benefit rare species of wildlife. Bird life is prolific, particularly during the breeding season, when countless seabirds seek out nesting sites, safe from predators on the high cliffs and bleak landscapes of the nearby islands. Calving seals value the isolation of the caves and rocky shores which lie at the base of the towering cliffs.

The spot is a suitable point from which to contemplate the next leg of your journey. The view north is across the open mouth of St Bride's Bay to St David's peninsula, some 15 k (9 mls) away. Ancient hills, standing above the plateau with the importance of mountains, guard the headland while off to the right, real mountains rise above a distant skyline, the Mynydd Preseli. Behind these on the coast lies your goal, the end of the path, and it is fitting to gaze at them since you are now approaching the halfway point of your adventure. The onward path is revealed in a more or less unbroken sweep to the right, only the stretch between St Bride's and Broad Haven being concealed by the protruding land mass of Nab Head to the east.

From the lookout, a downward path crosses the heath to a gate in Kensington's wall. Through the gate, turn left and go down the road to Martin's Haven beach.

Just past the toilets, look for a stone, faintly inscribed with a ringed cross, set into the wall on the left. It was discovered in the wall's foundations, and is evidence of the importance of Martin's Haven to early Christians.

Immediately before the beach the coast path is signed to the right, where steps take you onto low cliffs. They run more or less due east and gently rise above the splendid and often deserted beach of Musselwick Sands.

The path provides easy and generally level walking through lush grasses, bracken and occasional small copses of stunted trees and shrub, a contrast to the close cropped turf which was prevalent on the southern side of the peninsula. The cliff scenery is also very different; a more gentle panorama unfolds, displaying little of the dramatic chaos that the prevailing winds and waves have inflicted on the softer and more exposed cliffs behind. Nevertheless there is plenty of interest as the volcanic cliffs of Skomer recede to be replaced by the less resistant and thus more exploited sedimentary rocks at the back of St Bride's Bay. The transition to Red Sandstone is clearly evident in the cliffs at the northern end of Musselwick, and obvious underfoot when you eventually pass it.

Approaching Musselwick, the path crosses a drainage valley and track to the beach below, before regaining the more rugged heights to the north. Follow the then generally level path along the fringes of cultivation towards Tower Point and Nab Head.

Complex folding and multi-coloured rocks exposed by the relentless forces of nature draw the eye to the rugged cliffs below. The bold projection of Tower Point ahead has been fortified, and the ancient earthworks remain an impressive sight as you approach. The Nab, immediately beyond, has provided traces of even earlier occupation, its name deriving from knap, referring to the process of flint chipping which was carried out here around 5,000 BC. Flint was worked to produce a variety of implements before being traded with other settlements around the country. There is a blowhole to the north of the path as it cuts off the head of The Nab.

Across the neat fields to the right, the former seat of the Kensingtons stands in splendid isolation, its turrets and crenellations reflecting ostentatious Victorian fantasies rather than a need to repulse marauding natives. More lately it housed a convalescent and geriatric hospital and is now owned by a holiday company.

Walk onwards, the path gently losing height as it approaches St Bride's to drop onto the flat rocks at the head of the tiny cove.

St Bride's Church and the few surrounding buildings are picturesquely surrounded by a copse of woodland that nestles in gentle folds of encompassing rolling hills.

Chapter Eight

ST BRIDE'S to NEWGALE SANDS

19.2 kilometres (11.9 miles)

ST BRIDE'S

Many of the settlements and landings along this coast remember the name of an early saint, whose history owes as much to legend as it does to fact. St Bride's is no exception. The mystery of a mythological fire goddess known as Brig was personified in Brigid of Kildaire who was born around 450 AD. A remarkable woman, she became first a nun and subsequently an abbess, who with a subordinate bishop, jointly ruled a nunnery and monastery, brought together for common work and spiritual benefit. Although never leaving Ireland, her influence spread through Wales, south-western England and into continental Europe.

The present church, possibly thirteenth or even twelfth century, replaces an earlier building which stood closer to the sea. Coffins, or more properly,

St Bride's Haven

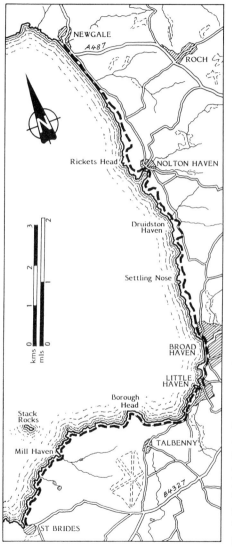

the stones used to line and cap the graves from the early churchyard, have been exposed by coastal erosion and can be seen in the low cliff just to the east of the limekiln.

After a stretch of low but rugged cliffs, the path climbs high beyond Mill Haven to run to the back of St Bride's Bay. The softer coal bearing rocks which underlie the coast to the north have been extensively exploited by drainage patterns, and consequently the walking there becomes strenuous with several steep sided valleys breaking through the cliffs. Erosion has in several places created instability, and caution is needed near friable edges. Thin seams of coal are exposed in places, and have been mined in the past. Remains of old workings are visible towards Newgale. There are some fine sandy beaches, and inevitably their accessibility has made them attractive to holidaymakers. However the intervening stretches are relatively unvisited.

Leave the beach to the east below a cottage, and climb gradually beside a stoned earth-bank, a mass of flowers growing from its crevices in the spring. Low twisting cliffs, revealing subtle changes of colour in the stone, guide you ultimately to Mill Haven. There, a flight of steps leads down a steep bank to the stream at the bottom.

MILL HAVEN

There is little obvious evidence of a mill, but a substantial stone wall stands adjacent to the stream. A few yards beyond is a limekiln, positioned to receive the limestone landed in the bay. Between the wall and limekiln is a curious depression, lined with rocks. It looks vaguely like the excavated foundation of a prehistoric dwelling. In fact, it is "eye", one of five sculptures collectively entitled "the eyes of the sea", an interpretation of the relationship between the land and sea by Alain Ayers executed in 1989. A carved erratic boulder lies alongside the coast path a short distance to the east and two further incised stones can be found by the path leading to Lower Broadmoor. The fifth was positioned beside the path to the west, but has either been removed or succumbed to the effects of the weather. Out to sea are the impressive Stack Rocks, their grey colour contrasting with the red tongues that run out from the cliffs below.

Climb from the bay, the onward path snaking in and out of a succession of tiny coves on its way to Borough Head.

Beyond Mill Haven are two Iron Age forts. The first, overlooking Mill Haven, is single banked and is more obvious in retrospect; the second is double banked, its height accentuated by scrub growing near the top.

Beyond Borough Head the path wanders through a grove of ever more abundant woodland, a lavish botanical contrast to the covering of grasses that cloaked the eastern side of the headland.

The luxuriant growth of oak, hazel, beech and others is draped with tentacles of ivy and honeysuckle, and owes its existence to the protection given by the headland behind, shielding it from the driving winter winds. In retrospect it almost gives the impression of an impenetrable rainforest, its verdant covering cascading down the cliffs to the sea; a rare sight along the path.

Abruptly, the path ends at a stile, beyond which is a lane. Turn

left (signposted Coast Path).

The lane carries the path around yet another Musselwick, the third such name on my maps during the course of the journey. Those with a propensity for such mental activities might like to determine the most used appellation along the path; no prizes for the winner though. I'm sure any answer would be much contested by reference to ancient maps and long forgotten local names! An even more prodigious feat would be to enumerate every fortification and ancient settlement encountered along the way.

Remain on the road for only a short distance. Beyond a road junction to Howelston, the path leaves on the left (signposted Coast Path). At first hedged, it quickly opens up to reveal Broad Haven ahead as it undulates towards its sandy beach.

Yet another fort is passed, this time overlooking Musselwick, although its form is not readily apparent. Later inhabitants of the area have mined coal from the cliffs below the fort. The coal is visible as black bands in the friable face of the cliffs. More coal can be seen as the path skirts Strawberry Hill on its descent towards Little Haven.

Walk on, the path weaving around tiny coves, whose apron of debris is composed of strangely cube-shaped boulders. The path then drops along field edges towards some houses, emerging onto a small promontory protecting Little Haven's one-time harbour. Follow it into the village.

LITTLE AND BROAD HAVENS

Little Haven is a picturesque and often bustling village, restrained by the steep hillsides of two converging narrow valleys. It was once a busy harbour, with ships docking to collect the coal that had been mined from the adjacent cliffs. A lifeboat was established in 1882, but following a decline in the amount of inshore shipping and the difficulty of raising a crew, it was closed in 1921. However in 1967 an inshore station was established, named the Little and Broad Haven Lifeboat and in 1992 it was given a new boathouse; perhaps an indication of the growing numbers of pleasure boats that sail in these waters.

Turn left onto the road and walk through the village. Leave along a lane on the left (signposted Broad Haven) and climb steeply above The Settlands before descending again to the coast at Broad Haven.

Variant: The Settlands

At low tide it is possible to walk along the shore between Little Haven and Broad Haven, thus saving both the effort of a climb and a walk along a road.

The views from the road are largely obscured by a bank and hedge, and possibly offer less interest than would an exploration of the cliffs below.

Broad Haven is one of three sandy beaches that look out across St Bride's Bay. Its massive indentation was formed as a consequence of the differential erosion of softer shales and coals which lie between the harder rocks of the peninsulas, bounding it to the north and south. Although a popular beach resort, the town has little of the character displayed by Tenby or Saundersfoot.

Walk either along the sand or promenade to the northern end of the beach, where there are some interesting rock formations. Join the coast road as it rises away from the shore, and almost immediately go left along a path (signposted Coast Path). It climbs onto the headland and follows the onward line of cliffs, occasionally at a respectful distance.

As the gradient eases the path comes close to the cliffs. Take a look back along their line. The Sleek Stone is an impressive, smoothly rounded cigar-shaped tongue of rock, protruding into the sea. To the south of it is my namesake Den's Door, a stack pierced by two arches. These cliffs are composed of thin shales and coal, and being friable, are subject to rapid erosion. As dramatic an example as any along the whole of the path is that taking place at Black Point, where a sizeable area of headland is slowly detaching itself from the main body of the cliff, taking with it an Iron Age fort. This particular slip has been under way since 1944, and access to the fort is now prevented by an ever widening gap.

A short distance on, the path rejoins the cliff edge, where there is a splendid view down to Haroldston Bridge, a particularly graceful natural arch through a tongue of rock curving out from the cliff; it culminates in a sloping shelf. More landslip is encountered to the north before, above the cliffs between Haroldston and Druidston Chins, the way ahead is barred and you are forced to turn right along a grassy track to the road.

The road follows the line of a prehistoric track that ran from Monk Haven near Dale to Porth Mawr on St David's Head. It avoided the dangers that a sea journey around the Marloes peninsula and across St Bride's Bay would have brought.

Turn left (signposted Coast Path) and follow the road to the Druidston Hotel. Just beyond, a path is indicated back to the coast (signposted Coast Path), which follows a stream downwards. At the bottom, the stream is joined by a second from the right to emerge onto the beach.

The shore is quite beautiful, with soft sand and a scattering of boulders, many of them erratics, laid out before a protective enclosure of cliffs. Those at the back of the beach are formed from unconsolidated glacial debris, left by the retreating glacier at the end of the last Ice Age.

Leave the beach with the second stream on your right and climb steps on the left (signposted Coast Path) to the top of the embankment to resume the onward journey. At Madoc's Haven the path originally maintained the high ground around a steep bank falling to the cliffs below; the path now drops to its base. After many years of closure the original line is still obvious, but you should resist temptation and take the descending track. Continue along the cliffs beyond to Nolton's Haven where you are brought back to the road beside a small chapel. Turn left and walk down the hill to the village.

Nolton's Haven was an important harbour in the eighteenth century from which coal, extracted from the many mines in the vicinity, was shipped. Stone was also quarried and used to make grindstones for flour and pepper mills.

Go onto the beach and leave by steps (signposted Coast Path) at its far corner to reach a path rising towards the open sea. The path picks its way through the debris of erosion and mining towards Rickets Head, a crumbling rocky outcrop connected to the mainland by a dipping shoulder. It then climbs steeply above old mine workings, from where there is a splendid view along Newgale Beach. The path eventually drops into a shallow valley, from the base of which protrudes a stark brick obelisk, an old chimney marking the site of Trefane Cliff Colliery.

Trefane was the largest colliery in the area, and from here shafts, inclining to depths of 90 metres (300 feet) under the sea, were worked for about 50 years until the pit closed in 1905. The wild setting and abandoned ruins evoke something of the harsh conditions that the miners must have faced in their industry.

When the tide is receding, you can scramble onto the beach and walk the remaining 2.5 kilometres (1.5 miles) along the sands to Newgale. Erosion has created some interesting effects in the southern cliffs. Beyond, they fall away, to be replaced by a high and austere shingle bank that contains the northern part of the beach. Otherwise climb away from the workings and follow a clear path through gorse, which eventually meets the road, dropping from the higher ground above. Walk ahead into Newgale.

Chapter Nine

NEWGALE SANDS to ST NON'S

16.7 kilometres (10.4 miles)

NEWGALE

Newgale presents a magnificent and unbroken stretch of sand, which runs in an uninterrupted stretch for over 3 kilometres (2 miles). On a bright and calm day it is as fine as any in Britain. However, facing directly out into St Bride's Bay, a gale can create a totally different picture. The high pebble bank, backing the sands in an almost straight line for much of its length, has been built by wind and wave action from boulders wrested from the coast to the west. Severe gales can push the sea over the top of the bar, as the residents of the Duke of Edinburgh inn, sheltering in its lee, can testify. A Duke of Edinburgh did indeed pass this way in 1882, and gave his name to the inn. Fourteen years later it was swept away, the landlady and her daughter barely escaping with their lives. Besides their skins, they also managed to rescue 20 sovereigns, and used them to open the present inn. It has been no less immune from the weather, but at least it still stands.

Our old friend Giraldus, when passing through Newgale in 1188, recalled that some 17 years earlier the wind had blown with such violence that the sand was blown from the beaches, exposing the sub-soil and revealing tree stumps of ancient forests, which still bore marks of the axes that had felled them. Giraldus also tells the story of a miracle that took place here. It appears that Saint Caradog, having followed the life of a hermit at St Ishmael's, had expressed a final wish to be interred at St David's. As the body was being carried across Newgale Sands on its final journey, a rainstorm occurred and the bearers took shelter, leaving the body in the open, covered only by a silken sheet. After the downpour they returned to find that miraculously it had remained dry. He offers no explanation but notes confidently that even today (that was 1171) the body is the cause of many miracles, and will continue to be so in the future.

At this point it is also interesting to note that the northern extent of Norman influence in Pembrokeshire was bounded here at Brandy Brook. Evidence lies in your companion, the map; notice that the names to the north are Welsh, whilst those in the southern part of the county are English. The

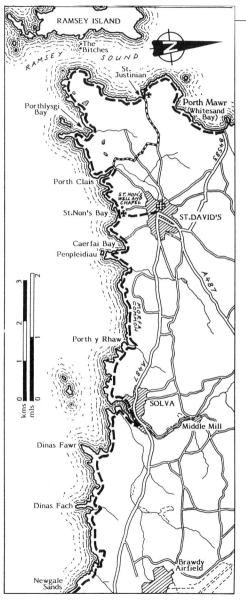

delineation can be traced across the map to the east.

The coast ahead is composed of older, harder rocks that have been sculpted by the elements to produce a tortuous delineation between the gently rolling hinterland and the ever active sea. The height of the cliffs is relatively constant, except where they have been gouged by the torrents of post-glacial streams to leave steep sided valleys, reaching back to a relatively flat interior. This has created an increasingly convoluted coastline which reveals new delights with each twist and turn. The periodic descents to sea level add further interest and combine to afford a greatly satisfying, if strenuous, walk that gradually leads you on to a wilder and more mysterious landscape.

If walking along the beach leave it for the road some 250 metres/ yards before the northern cliffs. Follow the road steeply up and look for a footpath beside a small garage on the left (signposted Coast Path) where the road bends sharply to the right. The path continues to climb steeply before dropping equally as abruptly into Cwm Mawr.

There is ample excuse to dally on the climb and enjoy the unobstructed vista of the beach and cliffs receding towards Broad Haven. However be prepared for a sudden and deafening assault on your ears. RAF fighters leave Bawdy Airfield just to the north, skimming the land before soaring out over the bay. On a busy day you can become convinced that there is personal malice in the actions of their pilots. However be assured that the onslaught is momentary and you will quickly pass from under their flight path. Reductions to the defence budget however threatens its future, and it may be closed.

Alternative:

For those who wish to postpone the expenditure of their energy for as long as possible, if the tide is out they may continue along the shore underneath the cliffs to the north of Newgale into Cwm Mawr before then leaving the beach to join the path.

Leave Cwm Mawr to regain the cliffs and walk ahead more easily on to Dinas Fach.

The rocks underfoot are coloured with streaks of mauve and purple, and are a precursor to the strikingly coloured cliffs further west. Beyond the boulder strewn base of the cliffs, clear green water washes over dark shoals, set amidst forests of seaweed and fields of sand. Ahead, beyond the secluded but accessible cove of Porthmynawyd, defiantly projecting into the sea is Dinas Fach, a rugged outcrop of rock that has resisted the waves. Beyond it is the even more substantial bulk of Dinas Fawr, along which the way appears to lie although in fact the path turns away at its base to follow the main line of cliffs. Both are ideally placed to be easily defensible and undoubtedly would have been used as prehistoric refuges, although little evidence remains today. If you have time, the detour to explore the headlands is repaid by views back to the cliffs.

The geological structure of the St David's peninsula has deposited veins of metal ore within the much fractured strata of its rocks. These have been known and worked since early times. As with the coal deposits encountered at the start of the walk and to the south of Newgale, they are much fragmented, and recovery on a large scale has never been economically viable. However, a number of small mines were worked around the coast, where the lodes were revealed in the cliffs and could be followed for short distances. One such area of industry was centred around Dinas Fawr, where deposits of galena, a lead ore but also containing significant amounts of silver, have attracted miners at various times since the 1600s. The deposits were said to be significant, although there is little evidence to suggest that they have been effectively exploited. Local tradition maintains that copper ore was also mined a short distance to the east of Dinas Fawr during the nineteenth century. Few traces remain, most of the addits have been sealed, and the restorative powers of nature have rounded the spoil heaps and hidden them beneath a mantle of vegetation.

Continue following the edge of the cliffs towards Solfach (Solva). As you approach the mouth of the estuary, the path turns away from the edge and avoids the point of Penrhyn to drop to the shore.

Two glacial meltwater valleys converge at Solfach, separated by the Gribin, a narrow dividing ridge, the tip of which was defended by an Iron Age earthwork. The nearer valley terminates in a shingle backed beach, its flat marshy bottom rising gently away. This secluded beach looks out to sea through a narrow rocky gap, which guards the entrance to Solfach.

Cross the beach and climb up the steep side of Gribin. A path from its crest gently descends along its tree-lined flank to the head of the estuary, where a bridge over the stream leads to the harbour car park.

Solfach is Danish for samphire, a squat fleshy plant of the parsley family, which can be cooked and eaten. It grows in the area, sprouting from crevices in the cliffs. Our own name for the plant derives from "sampier" - St Peter, the patron of fishermen, thus reinforcing an appropriate association for this old fishing village. It is a busy but attractive place, the more modern buildings overlooking the harbour from high above the western side of its valley. Although the entrance was not easy to navigate, its sheltered position gave protection not only from the sea but from the frequent raids that privateers used to make along the coast. The harbour developed to service trading ships, and limestone for the surrounding fields was imported to be burnt in kilns, four of which still stand at the water's edge in the shadow of the Gribin. Today in summer the estuary is filled with small yachts, which at high water are shepherded into orderly ranks by the gently flowing tide.

The first lighthouse to be erected on The Smalls, a dangerous group of rocks some 25 kilometres (16 miles) due west of Skomer, was prefabricated on the quayside here in 1775 before being shipped out to the rocks. Its wooden cabin, supported above the waves on pillars, survived for 80 years before being replaced by the present 43 metres (141 feet) high stone tower in 1861. Originally two keepers were stationed on the rocks, but during a tour of duty at the end of the eighteenth century one of them died. His companion, wishing to assert that there had been no foul play, placed his body in a box and lashed it to the outside of the structure. He tried to attract the attention of passing craft, but nobody arrived until the next relief ship, by which time he was in great distress. Since that time three keepers were always stationed on the rock until its conversion to automatic operation in 1987.

Walk down the estuary, leaving the quayside at its far end behind the one-time lifeboat station, and follow a path rising to a drive. Turn left, pass in front of a large white house and climb again through densely shrubbed hillside before joining the path from Solfach Uchaf at a gate. A field path beyond takes you once more onto the cliff tops. The path above Aber Llong is subject to continuing erosion, and it deviates ever more inland to remain on top of the cliff.

The walk along the headland offers splendid views of the coast in both directions. Fractured, crumbling cliffs and rocky outcrops stand above boulder strewn coves, and present a most forbidding coast. Further to the west the wrecks of three tugs that came aground in 1981 used to be visible at the low water mark. Constant pounding by storm waves has removed all trace other than the massive engine blocks, which in spite of their weight are in a different place each time I pass. However the cave below, Ogaf Tobacco, reputedly leading to the farm at Llanunwas, suggests that the very inhospitability of the cliffs was exploited by some of the more secretive traders operating along the coast.

Overlooking Porth y Rhaw at the far end of the headland, there is an outstanding promontory fort. A series of banks and ditches surround its flanks and the complexity of its entrance can still be traced. A more impressive view is to be had from the top of the headland to the west, as you turn to leave Porth y Rhaw.

After exploring the fort drop steeply down to Porth y Rhaw, where the stream at one time powered a mill. The climb on the other side is equally as steep, but there is then an easy walk over Morfa Common before again descending steeply to Caer Bwdy.

Shortly after crossing a gully running from Trelerew, look for a break in the cliffs. A wonderful purple fold in the sandstone runs along the base of the cliff, appearing somewhat like a mythical monster. In some lights it has an almost sinister appearance, as if lurking in wait for passing prey.

Caer Bwdy at one time also boasted a watermill; the ruins stand to the side of the path. Purple sandstone was quarried from the cliffs both in this bay and the next, Caerfai, to provide stone for the construction of the cathedral at St David's.

Again the path climbs, and on the next headland the builders of yet another fort took advantage of an isolated promontory to create a defensible position. Follow the line of the outer ditch before turning in to Caerfai Bay. At its head, a track crosses the path to the shore from the car park above; descent is not obligatory. The path continues easily ahead, along now lower but no less spectacular cliffs to St Non's Bay.

As you leave Caerfai, at a point where the path runs close to the cliff edge, notice a boulder to the right, whose flat top is inscribed with an apparently ancient symbol. The stone, an erratic, may be ancient but the carving dates back only to the 1980s.

Chapter Ten

ST NON'S to PORTH MAWR
12.7 kilometres (7.9 miles) See map p114

ST NON'S

The retreat at St Non's presides over a wild and rugged coastline, which portrays subtle beauties and changes of mood that accentuate the ancient mysteries and faiths in which this area is steeped. This spot has a religious significance pre-dating Christianity. A number of stones, part of a Bronze Age circle, stand in a field to the west of the retreat, and in the centre is the ruin of a chapel dedicated to St Non, who was the mother of St David. It is curiously aligned along the meridian rather than to the east, as is normally the case, and its age is uncertain. An inscribed stone from about the seventh century, now standing inside the chapel, was found built into the masonry. Tradition holds St Non's as being the birthplace of St David in 462. His nativity was accompanied by a thunderstorm, but a light is said to have miraculously shone over the spot, "as though God had brought the sun in front of the clouds".

Between the ruined chapel and retreat is the Holy Well. The spring which still flows from it is said to have appeared at the moment of St David's birth, but it could well be that it also had associations with the much earlier stone circle. Its waters are credited with healing powers, particularly for eye and rheumatic complaints. The attractive chapel in front of the retreat was built in 1934, shortly after the retreat was constructed. Its style is that of early chapels in the area, and the stone came from a priory, no longer standing, just to the north.

The cathedral city of St David's lies only 1.5 kilometres (0.9 mile) to the north, and unless time is really pressing, it is, as the Michelin guides would say, "worth a journey".

Addition: ST NON'S to ST DAVID'S 1.3 kilometres (0.8 mile)

There are two convenient routes, one following the lane away from the retreat, at the end of which turn right into Goat Street and then either cut through to the cathedral on the left or continue ahead up to the town cross.

Alternatively, a footpath runs from the east of the retreat, north across fields to the town, terminating at a track running behind a small housing estate. Turn right and then left, to walk through the estate onto Bryn Road, which runs parallel to the High Street. Cut through either to the right or left. The cathedral lies to the west, almost hidden in the base of a shallow valley.

ST DAVID'S

Tyddewi, "House of David", was established in an area already an important focus for the early Celtic Christian world because of its position on the coastal trade routes between Ireland, South West Britain and Brittany. St David, who had become an influential teacher and leader, settled here in about 550, and over the ensuing 50 years established a community. Hidden in the valley of the Alun, in order to reduce the risk of pillage by Viking raiders, a monastic church was founded. St David's significance to the Christian Church grew after his death, and Tyddewi itself became a place of pilgrimage, assuming such importance that it was said that three pilgrimages to St David's equated with one made to Jerusalem. This religious importance gave the place a popularity throughout medieval times, and the pilgrims, most of whom undoubtedly came by sea, brought with them trade and helped establish the many landings around the coast.

No trace of the original church remains; it was destroyed during a Viking raid about 1078. The present cathedral was started around 1180, and in common with such buildings has been added to and altered countless times over the succeeding centuries. Today's appearance owes much to Sir Gilbert Scott, who in the latter half of the nineteenth century supervised a substantial restoration programme to rescue the building, by then much neglected, from inevitable decay. A plain, unbuttressed, compact building, it is sited almost uniquely for a cathedral in a hollow that even its 38 metre (125 feet) square tower fails to significantly clear. Its facade does little to suggest the elegant richness of its internal construction and decoration.

Particularly notable is an unusual beamed roof from which carved bosses depend over the nave; it is of Irish oak, and was constructed around 1500. A splendid rood screen separates the nave from the choir, its magnificence emphasised by the fact that the floor of the nave rises from the west door to meet it. Carved misericordes from the late fifteenth century and a beautifully painted ceiling in the choir should also not be missed. Amongst the many tombs and memorials is a shrine dedicated to St Caradoc (whose body was brought from St Ishmael's) and of course the relics of St David.

Directly to the north of the cathedral, across the gently flowing Alun, stands the Bishop's Palace. Although a ruin, it remains substantial and still retains much of its former elegance; it dates from around 1280. The process of decay started only some 200 years after its building when the roof was stripped of its lead by the departing Bishop Barlow to fund, asserts local tradition, dowries for his five daughters; celibacy was not a clerical obligation in those days. The reformation sealed its fate, and it was not until the last century that work was carried out to stabilise the ruins.

A number of other ecclesiastical buildings are clustered around the cathedral, and the whole was surrounded for protection by an embattled wall. The present structure, of which substantial portions remain, dates to the fourteenth century. One of the four gateways still stands; you pass through it if approaching from the centre of the town. It is an imposing portal, standing above the cathedral from where, on a summer's evening, there is a splendid view as the rays of the setting sun lend a richness to the port-coloured stone.

St David's provides an excellent opportunity for accommodation and sustenance along a stretch of the coast where few amenities are immediately to hand.

Although over relatively low cliffs, the path from St Non's to Porth Mawr is rugged and demands effort. In compensation it affords some fine views, and in its short stretch contains as much variety in both geological formations and the flora and fauna that adorn it as any along the whole route. With luck you will also see some of the seals who favour the inaccessible coves of the mainland and the island, Ramsey, which lies just of the western coast.

On your return to St Non's continue west on a twisting path following the very edge of steep cliffs, before turning into the long narrow estuary of Porth Clais.

The steeply inclined slabs that buttress Trwyn Cynddeiriog are a favourite place for climbers, and you will often see teachers dangling small children over the edge on pieces of string. Are they being used as bait to lure aquatic subjects for use in a biology lesson or by the physics teacher to demonstrate some scientific principle? The mystery remains!

Porth Clais comes as somewhat of a surprise if you have not been walking with your nose in the map. Your attention becomes focused on the apparently continuing path ahead, for its narrow penetrating inlet remains hidden almost until you turn into it. However the extra walk is rewarded; its shrubby banks provide a contrast to the open coast and there are some well preserved limekilns beside the quay. St David is said to have been baptised here by Bishop Elvis, who had landed from Ireland especially for the occasion. The chapel which marked the spot and to which pilgrims would have journeyed was sited behind the harbour. The inlet, being the closest landing to the cathedral, developed to serve the community and both Irish and coastal small traders visited until well into this century. A gas works, now demolished, its site used as a car park, once provided St David's with gas, coal being landed at the quay.

Leave Porth Clais on the opposite side of the inlet. The path rises from behind two limekilns to head once more for the sea. It passes above low rocks, in which the weathering of the strata has produced fascinating patterns. Beyond, it turns into the more extensive Porthlysgi Bay.

Porthlysgi is a square, well sheltered bay with a high pebble beach, fed by a stream entering at its northern corner, where the path descends onto it. It takes its name from an Irish raider Lysgi who came here towards the end of the sixth century. The local chieftain Boia, whose settlement was at Clegyr-Boia about 1.5 kilometres (0.9 mile) to the north-east, attempted resistance but only got killed for his trouble.

Leave the beach and gain height quickly by a path alongside the bay, heading towards the open sea and the southern tip of the head.

Rocks and islets stand offshore, the sea swirling uneasily between them, and the headland beyond adopts a bleaker mantle. Ahead the mass of Ramsey Island, with its fractured satellites standing off its southern point, assumes an increasing prominence as you approach. Beyond Lower Treginnis, hidden in the undergrowth at the side of the path, are the remains of Melin Treginnis, a one-time corn mill. Pen Dal-aderyn on the tip of the point is distinguished as being the most westerly place on Pembroke's mainland coast. It marks the end of another section of the walk as you leave the vast sweep of St Bride's Bay behind to pass into Ramsey Sound, which opens before you as the path approaches higher ground. The narrow channel funnels the tide's ebb and flow. Water currents can reach 8 knots, and create a spectacular race flowing over the Bitches, the group of rocks lying towards the far side of the channel, behaving more like a river over a weir. Birds and seals floating on the water can drift below the point at an impressive rate.

Walk north alongside the Sound, the path twisting its way on to Penmaen melyn.

At Penmaen melyn there are two intriguing shafts sunk into the ground, almost on the very edge of the cliffs. The remains of stone walls add further mystery, and suggest some ancient lookout concealing an underground chamber. It is in fact all that remains of the Treginnis copper mine, which was worked from 1827. It was not a profitable venture and closed only 9 years later. A second shaft was sunk a short distance to the south above Porth Taflod, again searching for copper. That was worked until 1883 when, following a fatal accident suffered by one of the miners, it too was abandoned.

RAMSEY AND PORTHSTINIAN

Across the water lies Ramsey; its intrigue is heightened by the contradiction of its closeness and remoteness. Ramsey derives from the Norse, Rams-Øy, translated as Garlic Island, and has been settled since at least early Christian times. St Justinian, a hermit from Brittany and friend of St David, established a cell there. He was later murdered on the island for his criticism of monastic good living, and his body drifted to the mainland. Legend rather more colourfully suggests that he walked across the Sound, carrying his severed head. He was buried first at Porthstinian and later reinterred at St David's. It is also said that the bodies of 2,000 saints have been buried on the island.

Whatever the truth, the island remains an impressive outcrop. It is protected by forbidding cliffs that rise to 120 metres (400 feet) on its western coast, and are pierced at their base by deep and cavernous tunnels. These monolithic slabs, highlighted by the setting sun, acted as a guide for early sailors, navigating from Ireland. Extensive farming until 1968 has contributed to the island's varying landscape, which provides a variety of habitats for a wide range of flowers and both land and sea birds. Its slopes provide shelter for a prolific population of rabbits, and a herd of deer graze the hills. With binoculars, these can sometimes be seen from the mainland (the deer, not the rabbits), and in September forlorn cries of baby Atlantic seals, waiting on the rocky beaches for their mothers, drift across the water. The island, managed by the RSPB since the late 1960s and now owned by them, is a nature reserve. Visitor numbers are limited to 40 each day, but if you have the time a day spent in its exploration offers some of the finest cliff scenery in Pembroke. Equally rewarding are boat excursions around the island, which take you into the otherwise inaccessible caves and inlets where seals come ashore to birth and suckle their pups.

Porthstinian lifeboat station

Climb an outcrop of rock behind the ruin and follow the coast to Porthstinian, passing yet another, but less obvious banked earthwork, marked Castell Heinif on the map.

St David's lifeboat is housed spectacularly in a boathouse held high above the reach of the waves; its launching is quite a thrilling sight. St David's has had a lifeboat since 1869, although it first had to be kept in the town, in the garden of what is now the Old Cross Hotel, whilst the construction of its boathouse was being completed. However, following complaints from the village "elders" about "certain goings on" at night underneath the storage covers, it was temporarily moved to Porthlysgi; out of sight, out of mind, for I am sure the short walk down to the beach would have done little to deter the amorous intentions of the miscreants.

The second lifeboat to be stationed there, Gem, after successfully rescuing three sailors from their sinking ship in October 1910, was itself wrecked on the Bitches. Twelve of the crew, together with the three just rescued, were able to reach the rocks, but sadly the coxswain and two other crew members were drowned. Sydney Mortimer, a young lad of 18, rescued ten of the survivors. In recognition of his bravery he was awarded a silver medal and appointed as the new coxswain. The present boat, the seventh in the line, arrived in 1988 and is named for its benefactor, Garside. Its most recent claim to fame has been to feature in the BBC TV series Lifeboat. The trolley and winch at the top of the cliff are used to transfer supplies and equipment to the boats in the cove below.

The roofless chapel behind the lifeboat station is a sixteenth century replacement for an earlier Celtic chapel, strategically placed to receive thankful offerings from pilgrims for a safe voyage. Its association with St Justinian made it an object of pilgrimage in its own right.

Pass in front of the winch house, being careful not to trip over the cable, to continue towards Porth Mawr. Initially the path remains very close to the cliff top, having to divert inland occasionally to avoid areas of erosion.

The seemingly disproportionate number of stiles crossed in this area reflect old field patterns of small plots, enclosed by stone and earth embankments. These wonderful dividers generate a profusion of colour in the flowers that grow out of them during the spring and early summer. Modern post and wire fencing, an economic evil, has no such saving graces.

As you move around the point, you turn away from Ramsey and the open sea appears to your left. The infamous Bishops and Clerks, responsible for many shipwrecks, are progressively revealed as your line of sight moves south past Ramsey. They sweep from the North Bishop, some 5 kilometres (3.1 miles) due west of Penmaen Dewi in a line behind Ramsey, terminating at Em-sger or South Bishop.

Rounding the point eventually brings you to a sandy beach, Porthselau. From there the path climbs again before reaching Porth Mawr, eventually joining a gravel track which services a couple of houses built amidst the dunes behind the beach. A short distance further on, in front of "the Cabin", a fine example of minimalistic holiday accommodation, the path drops over a stile into the dunes. Walk ahead to a large car park above the northern end of the beach.

Chapter Eleven

PORTH MAWR to ABER DRAW

18.2 kilometres (11.3 miles)

PORTH MAWR (WHITESANDS)

Unashamedly a splendid holiday beach, Porth Mawr has something for everybody in its wide expanse of dune backed sand, terminating in cliffs and rocks to the north. In summer exciting excursions leave the beach to explore the cliffs and caves at the base of Ramsey and, as long as you can keep your boots dry when boarding, are a delightful excursion to add onto the journey.

The bay has close associations with Ireland; it is one of the sites from which, it is said, St Patrick sailed to undertake his ministry in Ireland, the country having been revealed to him by an angel. A sixth-century chapel used to mark the supposed spot, in the dunes just to the north of the car park. All that remains today is an inscribed tablet, hidden amongst the grass.

Links with Ireland have existed since the second millennium BC. In the Bronze Age traders landed copper and gold mined from the Wicklow Hills before taking it overland via the Mynydd Preseli to their settlements on Salisbury Plain.

Intrusions of hard volcanic rocks have been forced through the softer Ordovician shales and slates that more generally underlie the northern part of the county. Subsequent erosion has created a coastline of high precipitous cliffs, fractured and folded with a ruggedness that would not be out of place in the high mountains. It is a wild and lonely stretch of coast, and there are few trees to break its harsh lines, although much of the land is farmed to the cliffs. In places the path is steep and occasionally close to the edge of high cliffs, but the walking is good and the path for the most part maintains a respectful distance from the edge. Although there is a marvellous sense of remoteness, the road is never very far away. However, apart from perhaps an ice cream van at Abereiddi, there are no convenient facilities until you reach Trefin.

The path leaves to the north of the car park across a stile beside a telephone box. It then crosses the western flank of Carn Llidi

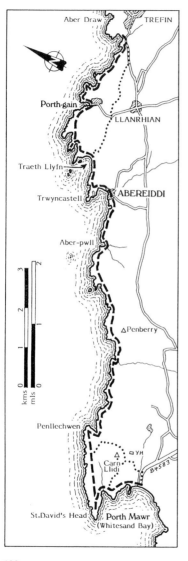

before dropping again to a little cove at Porthmelgan.

Carn Llidi, and its companions to the east, Carn Perfedd and Carn Penberry, justly deserve their affectionate dubbing as mountains. Together with the hills on Ramsey they have been a dominant feature on the skyline, breaking the low plateau throughout the walk around St Bride's Bay. From its foot, Carn Llidi remains a worthy goal, and for those overnighting at the youth hostel it is a wonderful spot to enjoy the setting sun.

The rock formations in the coves below the path never cease to delight the eye or excite the imagination. Porth Lleuog, separated from Porth Mawr by a rocky outcrop, is no exception. Parallel bands of rock run away from its head, one of them carrying a rocky pinnacle on top of a sloping platform, not unlike like the conning tower of a submarine.

As the path leads down towards Porthmelgan, in front of you on the skyline of St David's Head, starkly silhouetted against the sky, is Coetan Arthur, a Neolithic dolmen. Take a note of its bearing, for when you eventually arrive on the ridge its position is less obvious amongst the boulders and rocky outcrops, and it can be missed.

Cliffs below chapel at St Non's
St David's Head from Porthselau

Carn Pen Berry - west to St David's Head
Porth-gain

Cross a stream flowing down to Porthmelgan, and follow a clear path to the left which takes an easy line through the heather to the top of the hillside in front. It meets the ridge at Warrior's Dyke, and continues on towards the tip of the promontory.

ST DAVID'S HEAD

Warrior's Dyke is a stone bank fortification wall, still impressively partitioning the point from the remainder of the headland. It dates from the Iron Age, and enclosed a settlement. The foundations of several hut circles can be easily distinguished amongst the litter of boulders and outcrops of rock that lie along the ridge.

St David's Head provides a fine view out into the Irish Sea; indeed it is said that from the top of Carn Llidi behind you, it is possible to see the Wicklow Hills in Ireland. Although I don't doubt the veracity of the statement, I can't attest its truth. To the south there is a clear view along Ramsey Sound, which separates the island from the coast along which you have walked. The cliffs on the western tip of the island give some idea of the massive buttress the island presents to the open sea.

Beyond, the full sweep of the Bishops and Clerks are revealed. The group of rocks has always presented a considerable danger to coastal shipping. Following applications to Trinity House from the shipowners who used St George's Channel, a lighthouse was eventually established on Em-sger, the South Bishop Rock. It first came into use in 1839.

Retrace your steps to the stone rampart and continue north-east along an occasionally vague path following the crest of the ridge.

The Neolithic burial chamber, which presented itself so vividly on the skyline on the approach from Porthmelgan, now blends well amongst the jumble of boulders that scatter the headland; it stands to the right of the path.

The flat marshy valley dividing St David's Head from the mass of Carn Llidi to the right has been farmed since at least the Iron Age, and is almost certainly related to the settlement just visited on the headland. It is unique in Britain, and the small irregular field enclosures can still be traced along the sides of the valley. The signs are faint, and are best seen early in the year before the bracken has had a chance to conceal them beneath its profusion. More recently, the National Trust has introduced cattle to the area as part of a project to naturally manage the vegetation.

Walk onwards, making to the left of a rocky cairn and then gently drop towards the eastern tip of the headland.

The way ahead is now revealed. A mighty line of dark imposing cliffs guards the northern perimeter of Pembroke, and lead the eye along a line of isolated hills, standing out above a rolling plateau. The distant Garn Fawr and Strumble Head some 20 kilometres (12.5 miles) away obscure a more distant view, and establish themselves as the next landmarks along the route. However that distance, as usual is for the crow; your feet will have to take you a lot further.

At the far end of the headland the path turns in along the high cliffs above Gesail Fawr. From there an easy, twisting path rises and falls through heather, gorse and tussocky grass along the cliffs and hillsides, towards the dominant mass of Carn Penberry ahead.

This stretch of the Pembrokeshire coast is wild and lonely, and is in many ways perhaps the most beautiful.

Ahead, Penberry appears to rise straight from the sea. The path climbs steeply, high above the flanking cliffs to cross its shoulder, from where there are superb views in both directions. The way is then much easier as it drops towards Castell Coch, a desolate outcrop, whose shattered cliffs resolve as you approach.

Stark cliffs abruptly mark the limit of cultivation, and contrast with a plaid of neatly walled and manicured fields on the rolling land behind. The path snakes above their smooth flanks; below they terminate in a chaotic mass where the sea constantly wells at their feet. There are many small bays, with rocky shores well protected by high buttresses rising above. In early autumn these provide many opportunities to watch seals, lazily bobbing on an offshore swell or coming ashore to feed their pups, who lie almost hidden in the rocks below. I have often wondered, whilst sitting watching them, who is providing whom with the spectacle. Many appear as interested in us as we are in them.

Castell Coch's (coch means red) natural defences have been enhanced by the construction of a double banked earthwork to defend the promontory. As you approach, fractured rocks and pinnacles assume something of a ruined medieval castle, guarded by outcrops of rocks protruding from the water below. Erosion and slate quarrying have both contributed to create a confused picture. Below the path to the east of the outcrop is an impressive blowhole connecting with a cave in the cliff. Its base is blocked by the debris of broken slate.

The path continues easily on springy turf outside the perimeter of cultivation. At Aber Pwll drop steeply to the head of a rocky beach before climbing away just as abruptly to the cliff tops beyond. There is then an easy walk to the beach at Abereiddi.

Aber Pwll is a tiny shingle-beached cove. It is a wonderful spot to sit and watch the sea. Funnelled by rocky walls on either side, the energy of incoming waves is focused on the beach. The rising swell traps air inside caves and crevices at the base of the cliffs, creating a deep "booming" sound that competes with the crash of water amongst the rocks. On the cliffs between Aber Pwll and Abereiddi there is yet another Iron Age fort, and your now practised eye will easily spot the line of fortification as you cross through the defence.

The cliff path ends just to the south of Abereiddi beach, where a stile leads to a narrow lane. Turn left (signposted Coast Path) and follow it to a junction. Again turn left and follow the road to the car park above the beach.

ABEREIDDI

These cliffs are of Ordovician slate, and where it is exposed, weathering often makes it friable and easily cleaved along its grain. As the deposits were being laid down some 450 to 500 million years ago, the bodies of graptolites, ancient sea creatures, became embedded in the fine mud. Their fossil remains are abundant in the shales in this area, and a few minutes exploring the debris below weathered outcrops will usually reward you with an odd example or two.

The settlement of Aber-Eiddy grew to prominence as a result of the exploitation of the slate in its cliffs. By the middle of the nineteenth century it was exporting slates to roof buildings in the rapidly growing industrial towns of England and Wales. Originally the slate was exported directly by boat from the beach to the railhead ports around the Bristol Channel and then on across the country. Later the quarries around Porth-gain, the next village to the east, began to develop. A 3 mile narrow gauge tramway was constructed along the shallow valley behind Ynys Barry to take the slate from Aber-Eiddy to the harbour there. Aber-Eiddy's quarries lie to the north of the beach and had been opened to the sea to create a small harbour. However at the beginning of this century they were flooded one night during a storm. They were never reopened and now lie abandoned, leaving nature to slowly set about removing their harsh outlines. A couple of fishing boats still take advantage of the harbour, now called the Blue Lagoon.

A row of crumbling quarrymen's cottages stand in a line away from the

Old quarry workings at Aber-Eiddy

beach. Together with the foundations of the quarry stores and site offices on the hillside overlooking the workings, they are all that remain of the little community that once thrived here. The hamlet was inhabited until around 1930 when it was finally abandoned. Two stories describe its end. One relates that the grocer, who periodically visited the village with his horse-drawn cart to sell provisions, unwittingly carried in typhoid. This spread rapidly through the small community with fatal consequences. The other story tells of a storm bringing waves over the back of the beach and drowning the houses. Possibly they both had a part to play in creating the lonely epitaph that remains today.

Take a path behind the end of the cottages, heading towards some ruined buildings and quarries at the northern end of the beach. It then divides, the left path going into the quarries and by which you must return if you go to investigate, whilst the right hand path climbs to the cliffs above.

The path avoids the headland of Trwyncastell, separated from the main cliffs by a moat-like gulf. The prominent tower on the headland is a navigation mark, located to assist the boats that came to transport the slate from the quarries.

An easy walk meanders around the bleak and often windswept perimeter of Barry Island. The path takes a more direct line, avoiding the many promontories that protrude from the coast. It arrives eventually at the top of the cliffs above Porth-gain, where a flight of steep steps descends to the harbour.

Intrusive erosion of the western flank of Ynys Barry has produced a succession of bays backed by sheer cliff walls. The first, Traeth Llyfn, is accessible, at one time by a flight of steps cut into the rock during the Second World War by Italian prisoners. However erosion eventually made it unsafe, and they have recently been replaced by a metal staircase. It may be practical, but I'm sure Prince Charles would have a word or two to say about it.

PORTH-GAIN

Our own intrusions on the landscape merely continue the traditions of our forefathers. The abandoned quarries, tramways and buildings that abound on Ynys Barry and around Porth-gain stand as a testament to nineteenth and early twentieth century industry and opportunism. The sedimentary slate of the headland contains an intrusion of granite, which around the edges has decomposed to produce a fine quality clay. Quarries were dug to produce roofing slate, granite building blocks, road sets and stone. Clay was also dug for the manufacture of bricks. The developing industrial towns brought prosperity to Porth-gain and the harbour was rapidly developed to accommodate the flotilla of boats arriving to carry away the stone. A further boost came at the beginning of this century with the development of the automobile, which required smooth roads to run on. The hillside above the quay was encased in brick, creating giant hoppers to store crushed granite, which was needed for the construction of the new roads.

The main disadvantage of Porth-gain, from which it began to suffer, was its relative isolation. Large scale transport was only possible by sea and the village began to feel the effects of competition from quarries serviced by the expanding rail network. Plans were made to link with a proposed extension of the London North Western Railway to St David's, but this never materialised, and the Great Depression between the two World Wars hastened the decline that competition had started. By 1931 the quarries and processing plants had closed down and the promise of industrial prosperity faded as quickly as it had begun. It is sobering to reflect that much of the beauty along the Coast Path, and indeed of the Kingdom as a whole, owes as much to the chance of industrial fortunes as it does to the hand of nature.

What remains at Porth-gain is an attractive harbour behind which is an impressive (now restored) warehouse. Along the valley, placed to enjoy the afternoon sun, are a few houses and an interesting old pub, the Sloop Inn, which proudly displays that its origins date back to 1743 AD, yes AD - for the avoidance of doubt, my legal friends would say. Fishing boats frequent the quay, and the brick tunnels behind are used to store equipment. The huge brick hoppers, and the remains of the buildings and tramways that lie behind, provide plenty of interesting diversions, but take care as old workings and buildings can be dangerous.

Leave the harbour, climbing towards a navigation marker whose pair was passed below the path on the approach to the inlet. The path continues around the headland.

There is an impressive succession of coves at Gribinau and, beyond, a chasm separates the massive detached stack of Ynys-fach from the coast.

After a short but sharp dip above Pwllcrochan, field paths lead on to the farm Swyn y Don. Skirt the buildings and emerge over a stile beside its entrance from the road. Turn left (signposted Coast Path) and walk to the bottom of the hill where there is a small bridge over the stream at Aber Draw.

The village of Trefin lies a further 0.8 kilometre (0.5 mile) along the road where there is food and lodging for those who need it. Otherwise the path returns to the coast.

Chapter Twelve

ABER DRAW to PWLL DERI
15.6 kilometres (9.7 miles)

The coast ahead loses none of its ruggedness, and the "mountains" of St David's Head behind are replaced by the ever-growing prominence of Garn Fawr. However, although the path rises to meet it, culminating in an exhilarating high ridge, almost 2 kilometres (1.25 miles) long, that leads to its very foot, there is no compulsion to ascend. The path along this section is good throughout, although there is again an occasional requirement for extra effort. As along the last stretch there are no convenient facilities, and apart from a few houses at Abercastle and the youth hostel at Pwll Deri, there is nothing immediately to hand.

The substantial but roofless ruin beside the bridge at Aber Draw is an old watermill. It was still in use towards the end of the last century. Inside are the abandoned millstones, which were employed to grind the grain into flour. A path runs from the side of the mill to a quiet and delightful shingle beach below.

The coast path leaves the road immediately beyond the bridge (signposted Coast Path) to climb onto the headland and follow the much indented coastline towards Castell Coch.

The climb from Aber Draw gives an opportunity to look back along the cliffs you have just walked. From the headland, the line of sight back to Ynys-fach shows it to be pierced by an arch, fashioned with true Norman elegance.

Similar in many ways to the coastline north of Abereiddi, these westward facing cliffs have been gouged out into a succession of bays, as the sea has exploited weaknesses in the steeply inclined beds of slate and shale. The constant meandering of the path provides wonderful views into the inaccessible coves below. At the end of summer many are home to seals, their pups often barely distinguishable from the scattered rocks that populate their floors. Rocky stacks and narrow arêtes survive amidst the confusion, but their triumph will only be temporary, as the ongoing erosion around Pwllwhiting demonstrates.

Castell Coch, like its namesake some 12 kilometres (7.5 miles) back along

135

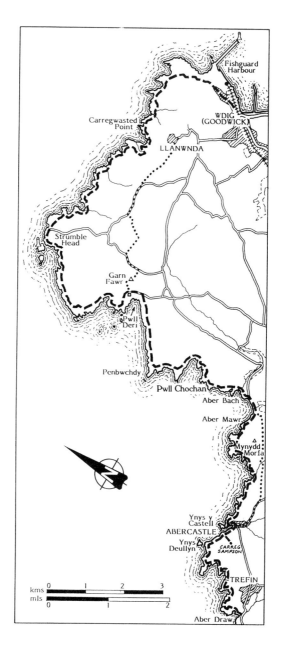

the path, has been exploited as an Iron Age defence; two lines of embankments can be traced across the neck of the promontory. The cliffs below are being dramatically undercut, allowing the waves to wash in underneath the "castle". To the north, erosion has separated the mass of Ynysdeullyn from the cliffs, the intervening space occupied by a smaller but craggier unnamed stack, impressively fashioned into something of a miniature Tryfan look-alike. Beyond, the coast runs on to Strumble Head, Garn Fawr asserting its dominance over the undulating countryside.

Approaching Aber Castle, the contours of the land at first conceal the long narrow cove that extends inland to form the harbour. As the perspective changes, the consequential diversion and loss of height that is entailed is slowly revealed.

Although highlighted here as an addition, the extra effort involved in making a detour to visit Carreg Sampson hardly makes it worth ignoring. It is an excellent example of a Neolithic burial chamber and lies just a short distance to the south of the path.

Addition: CARREG SAMPSON

Two paths to the dolmen are signed, one immediately before

Carreg Sampson dolmen

the coast path descends towards the mouth of Aber Castle and the second a few metres/yards beyond, where the path skirts a pebbled cove to enter the estuary. Either will lead you across the fields to the burial chamber about 250 metres (300 yards) away at the top of a shallow valley behind the cove. After inspecting it return to the Coast Path to continue walking to Aber Castle.

Carreg Sampson is a Neolithic burial chamber, around 5,000 years old, and is perhaps the most impressive encountered along the path. When originally built, the structure would have been encased within a boulder heap, and the whole covered with earth. What you see is the central chamber. Legend has it that the capstone was placed in position by Sampson, using only his little finger. That finger is supposed to be buried on Ynys y Castell, the rocky island opposite guarding the entrance to Aber Castle. It is also possible that "Sampson" may in fact refer to "Samson", a contemporary of St David whose association with Caldey was mentioned as we passed by that island.

The coast path drops onto rocks above the waterline to lead up the narrow estuary into the tiny village.

As you walk up the estuary, notice that two of the bollards beside the path, now employed as boat moorings, are in fact cannon. The little inlet has been used as a harbour for centuries, and its Welsh name Cwm Badau appropriately describes it as the "Bay of Boats". The limekiln at the end of the path is in particularly good condition, and the ruin overlooking the harbour on the opposite bank was once a grain store.

A concrete path leads across the marshy ground behind the beach, where the signed Coast Path leaves to gently climb behind the former grain store to the headland. The way turns in front of Ynys y Castell towards Aber Mawr, the next beach along the coast.

Heavily fractured cliffs dominate this stretch, their bases gnawed by the sea to create splintered pinnacles, crevices, holes and arches. Shattered remnants of razor sharp stacks and outcrops of rock fringe the whole of this jagged stretch, creating a most fearsome spectacle. The cliff wall is broken by a deep narrow valley at Pwllstrodur. Its steep sides provide enough shelter from the wind to allow a few trees and shrubs to grow around a stream which flows onto a shingle beach beyond. Two successive peninsulas project from the headland below Mynydd Morfa, and although the path ignores them, cutting across their bases, they give fine views along the coast. The second,

Penmorfa, has been fortified, and embankments running parallel to the path can be identified, the outer (nearer) line being emphasised by a field wall. It too is named Castell Coch, the last to be so dubbed along the trail.

Follow the path to the head of the beach at Aber Mawr, where it continues along the shingle bar and out at the far side to the end of a narrow lane. There, to the left, is a stile (signposted Coast Path) over which a short walk across a low crumbling cliff leads to the similar but much smaller bay of Aber Bach.

ABER MAWR

Both bays are backed by delightfully wooded valleys that reach into the hillside behind, almost at right angles to each other. The pebble bars along the high water marks that restrict drainage and thus make the valleys behind marshy were only thrown up in 1859 when a severe storm fell upon the coast.

In today's peace and tranquillity it is hard to believe that half way through the nineteenth century Brunel chose Aber Mawr as an alternative to Wdig (Goodwick) as his Irish seaport. Considerable preparatory work was undertaken to lay out the course of the railway and harbour before a new decision to use the Milford Haven waterway instead was made. The construction was abandoned and the workmen turned their attentions to Neyland.

The lane to the east of Aber Mawr which now ends abruptly above the beach, at one time used to continue across it and on to Aber Castle. Erosion has caused its disappearance.

Each atmospheric nook and cranny along this coast seems to have its own legend, and Aber Bach is no exception. A fisherman is supposed to have caught a mermaid here and carried her to his cottage at Treseissyllt, about 1 kilometre (0.6 mile) to the north-east. She eventually managed to escape, leaving behind a curse that was not broken until 1960, that no child would ever be born in the house.

Cross the beach and leave by a path, between a limekiln and a roofless ruin, that climbs steeply away. Having regained height, the route to Pwll Crochan is an easy walk over stony ground.

The cliffs around Pwll Crochan have been subjected to severe folding, revealed in the buttresses and arêtes running from them. At the far end of the bay erosion has created a cave underneath a sharp anticlinal fold. The beach, overshadowed by dark and dripping cliffs, looks uninviting and access is to be discouraged. I do remember, however, spending almost the whole of a delightful afternoon watching from the cliffs a baby seal, who with a total lack of inhibition was playing in one of the rock pools below.

The path climbs away above Pwll Crochan, only to lead steeply down and then up again across a small gully to the north. A stretch of easier walking follows, after which there is a more gradual pull onto a cliff-top ridge. This runs in an almost straight line north-east from Penbwchdy Head. Walk on, enjoying the view, until the path finally ends at a narrow lane above Pwll Deri.

The path stays on the landward side of the crest, where the ridge slopes more gently inland. There is a delightful panorama across a rich and productive countryside. Heather and gorse profusely cover the top of the ridge, and provide shelter for a surprising variety of flowers, even in this exposed position. These cliffs, at around 125 metres (400 feet) high, are the highest so far encountered along the Path and provide a wonderful retrospective view along the coast to St David's Head. In the early evening the low shaft of light from the setting sun can fall onto the water below to create a thousand scintillating jewels. In front the cliffs behind Pwll Deri are subordinated by Garn Fawr which rises almost as steeply behind, reaching 213 metres (700 feet) at its summit. The tiny white building sitting in its midst is Pwll Deri youth hostel; realising that the Coast Path passes behind it gives some idea of the scale of the cliffs.

Turn left into the lane (signposted Coast Path) and walk to the entrance of the youth hostel some 350 metres/yards along.

Pwll Deri is justly noted as one of the beauty spots along the Pembroke Coast, although its popularity perhaps owes as much to its accessibility to the motorist as it does to its natural setting. Nevertheless it is a wonderful spot, looking back along some 20 kilometres (12.4 miles) of the most dramatic coastline in Wales. Its enchantment inspired a poem of Dewi Emrys, a Welsh writer, and he is remembered in a memorial at the side of the road, close to where the Coast Path emerges.

Dewi Emrys 1879-1952
A HINA'R MEDILIE SY'NDWAD ICHI
PAN FRCH CHI'N ISHTE UWCHBEN PWLLDERI

and these are the thoughts that come to you when you sit above Pwllderi

Chapter Thirteen

PWLL DERI to WDIG (GOODWICK)
14.8 kilometres (9.2 miles) See map p136

The walk from Pwll Deri to Wdig follows a wild and deserted coast, preserving the same sense of remoteness and solitude that much of the coast since St David's has generated. Most of the farmhouses are placed well inland, or tucked into the valleys that gently fold the headland, leaving the seaward fields to the hardier crops and sheep that seem to thrive on this landscape. The path is in places rough, and again occasionally demanding on the legs, but clear throughout.

GARN FAWR

For those with energy and time to spare, the short but steep climb to the summit of Garn Fawr is well worth the effort. The footpath leaves the road to the right, utilising the access to Tal-y-gaers, opposite the youth hostel. The summit was enclosed as an Iron Age settlement and the remains of some of the stone walls can still be seen, although much of the site is overgrown. By the summit trig point, expertly carved into the rock is a compass rose and, beyond, taking full advantage of the hill's position, is the ruin of a lookout used during the First World War. It bears the names of the Commander and his Deputy, together with the builders, J.J. Thomas & Pritchard.

Turn left into the youth hostel drive but immediately leave on the right along a path (signposted Coast Path) descending to the coast. A winding path takes you around the coast to Strumble Head where it ends at a small car park above the lighthouse. The way is generally easy, although there are two or three steep pulls, necessitated by the path crossing valleys, which are out of all proportion to the streams that run in them.

Ahead Ynys y Dinas, protruding into Pwll Deri, is not quite an island, and was an ideal location for the Iron Age fort built upon it. Only minimal earthworks were necessary in order to complete the defence of the narrow neck of land connecting it to the mainland. The vertically cracked horizontal strata of its eastward cliffs give it more the appearance of an immense man-made wall than the product of nature. A track leads from the main path down to cross the thin peninsula onto the mound. The digression to explore it is well repaid with views back into the dark recesses of Pwll Deri, its inaccessibility encouraging seals onto its rocky shores.

At the back of Porth Maenmelyn, a steep flight of steps passes sinisterly through a gash in the cliff wall on its way to the beach, suggesting a smuggler's route from the deserted hills behind. The steps and gash were actually cut at the turn of the century to give a previous owner of what is now the youth hostel access to his boat, which he kept in the cove below. There is no access, the way is barred and the bottom section of the steps is much eroded. The brick building above the path at Pen Brush and occasional concrete tracks that mysteriously appear from underneath the gorse banks beyond remain from the war.

Beyond the summit of Pen Brush the path winds on to Strumble, the lighthouse periodically appearing through intervening folds in the land, acting as much as a beacon for the land traveller as it does for the mariner. The lighthouse sits on a small flat topped island and when gently veiled with sea mist gives the impression of a baby's first birthday cake. It dominates Ynysmeicl (St Michael's Island) and was built in 1908 to guide shipping from Ireland around Strumble Head and into the newly opened Fishguard Harbour, sheltering behind its eastern flank. Operation is now automatic and is controlled from the main station at St Ann's. The chain of rocks and little islands that extend from it across Carreg Onnen Bay create a delightful lagoon.

Walk along the road away from the lighthouse. After some 300 metres/yards it bends to the right, the signed Coast Path leaving to the left. The path follows an easy route around a succession of bays and headlands, briefly dropping to the shore at Porthscian before eventually arriving at Carregwastad Point.

CARREGWASTAD POINT

Carregwastad was the landing site for the last invasion of Britain. A memorial stone was erected to mark the centenary of the event and reads:

1897

CARREG GOFFA CLANIAD Y FFRANCOD CHWEFROR 22 1797

and below in English

MEMORIAL STONE OF THE LANDING OF THE FRENCH FEBRUARY 22 1797

At a period in their history when the French were falling out with just about everybody in Europe, the revolutionaries held a special dislike for the English who had voiced support for the French crown. A plan conceived by General Hoche, a one time corporal to land three forces, one in Ireland, one in Tyneside and the third in Bristol, was designed to encourage popular revolt and precipitate civil war in this country. It would appear that everything that could go wrong, did. His forces to Ireland and Tyneside were beset by storm and shipwreck, never reaching their objectives. The final group, led by an Irish American, William Tate, was forced from its preferred landing by unfavourable winds and arrived off Carregwastad during the night of 22 February 1797. Accompanied by an army of 600 soldiers and 800 convicts with minimal provisions and no shelter, Tate was ill prepared. The unruly band raided nearby farms for food, but instead discovered a cache of liquor recently "rescued" from a shipwreck by the local people, and ended up getting drunk.

The alarm was raised and Lord Cawdor of Stackpole responded to command the repulse, bringing some of his own men to join others from Fishguard. After a brief skirmish which resulted in only minimal losses to the French, Tate surrendered to Cawdor at the Royal Oak inn in the centre of Fishguard, and so ended the adventure. As a more individual footnote, there is a memorial in St Mary's churchyard at Fishguard to Jemima Nicholas, who at the age of 47 and armed only with a pitchfork captured a dozen of the Frenchmen.

From the monument the path drops into Cwm Felin, a delightfully wooded valley and then regains the high ground around the back of Aber Felin. Beyond, it takes a more direct route, cutting off a succession of minor promontories that reach out from the eastern end of the headland. Above Anglas Bay the path turns its back on the coast, following field margins to head south, over an unkempt gorse covered common above Fishguard Bay. Finally, after passing some rather run-down allotments, the path terminates at the end of a street at Harbour village.

A series of coves below the eastern slopes of Aber Felin provide a last opportunity for seal-watching before the path returns once more to civilisation. The tip of Pen Anglas, conveniently avoided by the path since it involves 60 metres (200 feet) of descent and re-ascent over rough heather, is noted for the polygonal jointing of the basalt that has occured during solidification from the molten state.

GOODWICK HARBOUR

There is a fine view from the path over Fishguard Bay. Ahead, the town of Fishguard occupies the hill overlooking the main harbour, and behind, tucked away into the Gwuan estuary, is the picturesque Old Town with its own harbour.

The monumental North Breakwater was built to protect the developing harbour at the turn of the century. 1.6 million tons of rock were used in its construction, all of which was quarried out of the cliffs below Harbour village, the excavated area being subsequently used as a platform for the harbour rail terminal. The harbour was finally opened in 1906. An initial plan to develop a port here for the Irish trade had been aborted some 60 years earlier as a result of the Irish potato famine. During that time Neyland had been built, but having insufficient depth of water to accommodate the new generation of larger ships, was unable to attract the more prestigious North Atlantic trade. Fishguard provided the solution with an easily accessible bay giving a draft of 30 metres (100 feet). It was also directly connected to the Great Western Railway network. For a short time it achieved supremacy, attracting visits from the Mauretania and Lusitania, but the First World War and the development of Liverpool as a major port brought the dream to an end. Irish ferries still sail to Rosslare; you can watch them coming in at noon and returning again in the afternoon.

Harbour village was built to house employees of the Great Western Railway who were employed in the harbour terminus at the bottom of the cliff. To make way for its construction, a group of Neolithic burial chambers was destroyed and now only two remain, located behind the houses to the west.

Walk past the houses and then down New Hill into Wdig (Goodwick). At the bottom, cross the main road and continue down Station Hill past the Rose and Crown to The Parrog, the promenade running at the back of Wdig beach.

Chapter Fourteen
WDIG (GOODWICK) to NEWPORT
20.4 kilometres (12.7 miles)

The ensuing 3 kilometres (1.9 miles) skirt the urbanisation of Fishguard before passing the old town of Abergwaun to then regain the open cliffs. Beyond, the walking is energetic as the path is forced up and down by high cliffs that rise into the hinterland, or to negotiate deep thickly wooded valleys. Dinas Island, about halfway between the towns, offers a choice of route, both possessing attractive qualities. Beyond, the scenery is no less spectacular before the path gently loses height and turns in to Newport's wide estuary.

WDIG (GOODWICK) AND FISHGUARD

The names Goodwick and Fishguard derive from the Norse "Wdic" and "Fisgard", which mean an anchorage and fish-yard respectively, and give the places a history dating back to the eighth century. The Neolithic relics passed behind Harbour village, however, indicate that settlement in the area dates back at least to around 3,000 BC. Modern Wdig and the Upper Town only developed with the promise of prosperity brought by the railway and new harbour, but the Old Town of Abergwaun had been a prosperous herring and trading port since the sixteenth century. Its old dwellings and harbour buildings clustered around the quayside have retained their distinctive character, which attracted the filmmakers of Moby Dick *and* Under Milk Wood *to use it for location scenes.*

The coast's proximity to Ireland gave it the honour of being the departure point for the first flight across the Irish Sea. Denys Corbett Wilson took just 100 minutes to fly to Enniscorthy from a field near Llanwanda on 22 April 1912. At one time there used to be a small memorial plaque marking the field, but I have been unable to locate it in recent years.

Walk to the opposite end of the promenade. Immediately beyond a bridge under which Goodwick Brook gains freedom in the sea, a signed footpath to Fishguard Old Town leaves the road on the left and climbs the hill to emerge at a small car park. Turn left and follow a tarmac path around the headland cliffs below Upper

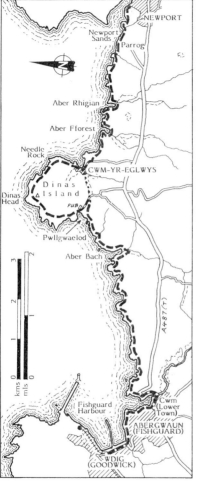

Town. If you wish to go into the town, after passing Saddle Point there are a number of paths on the right leading into the centre.

The path eventually meets a short street, Bank Terrace. Continue past the houses to its end, where a lane runs down to the beach (signposted Coast Path). Go left and, after passing two limekilns, take a tarmac path on the right to the harbour car park. Cross it and turn left onto the main Cardigan road, the A487. Follow this through Abergwaun and out up the hill. Towards the top a signed path leaves through a gap in the wall on the left. Follow this to Castle Point.

If you can afford a few minutes to linger, wander around the old harbour which dates from the eighteenth century. Busy fishing and trading fleets operated out of the port and the tall building beside the car park on the western bank of the river, now partly used by the Sea Cadets, is one of the former warehouses. The dwellings clustering at a respectful distance behind the quay on the eastern bank form a delightful picture. The warning notice on the harbour concerning high tide is no idle threat, as spring tides can wash the doorsteps of the surrounding houses.

Castle Point is the site of an eighteenth century fort, built on what was originally an Iron Age promontory defence. Although small it is worthy of exploration. Apart from some standing lengths of wall and a doorway, there is a small, two roomed building with its barrel roof intact. The fort was built following an attack on the town by Paul Jones, a Scottish born American, who during the American War of Independence became a Commander in the American Navy. He had captured one of the town's trading ships and threatened to bombard the town if he was not paid a ransom of 500 guineas. Although he was paid off, the town was determined that they should not suffer a similar fate in the future, and built the fort on the headland to deter those with similar intentions.

The path eastwards is generally quiet and, after dropping almost to the beach at Pwll Landdu, climbs above cliffs that reach high up the flanks of Carn Ffrân and Carn Geli to the right. You eventually emerge over a stile into Fishguard Bay Caravan Site, which occupies the headland of Penrhyn Ychen, formerly a lookout post during the First World War.

The cliffs, topped in heather and gorse, rise ahead, their thinly bedded shales much exploited to leave a fringe of jagged outcrops, washed by the waves below. Particularly striking is Needle Rock, which is best seen in retrospect from where the path dog-legs outwards above Aber Richard, giving an unobstructed view of the cliff line. The Needle is pierced through at its base by an arch, its "eye". In front, the view is dominated by Dinas Head, its massive northern tip rising 142 metres (463 feet) out of the sea.

Walk in the direction of the site shop to turn right along the main drive. Go left at the top perimeter of the field, where the path then resumes over a stile in its corner. The way is signposted Coast Path throughout. A hedged path, giving glimpses down sheer cliffs to the confused debris in the coves beneath, takes you towards the variously named Aber Hes'cwm or Aber Bach. It there turns inland along a field perimeter to terminate at a narrow lane. Turn left (signposted Coast Path) and then leave through a gate on the left (signposted Coast Path), where the lane makes a sharp right turn. Follow the track down through trees to the beach.

Typical of the complex structure of this coast is the folded strata in the cliffs below Penrhyn Erw-goch, which make an interesting study. Similar folding appears in the cliffs surrounding Aber Hes'cwm; the cliffs in the eastern corner of the bay are particularly fascinating. The bay is a delightful surprise, along this otherwise rugged line of battered cliffs. Hidden within a deep bay and protected by high cliffs, Hes'cwm is a quiet beach of grey sand and pebbles backed by a verdant valley. The stream used to drive a mill situated amongst the trees up-stream.

A well built bridge over a stream carries the path to the beach; it leaves at the opposite end. After a short pull, the gradient eases and the path drops behind the crescent shaped bay of Pwll Gwylon, where there is access to the shore alongside a stream. Climb high again above the almost vertical cliffs that separate it from Pwllgwaelod. It is then downhill over a grassy bank to walk the final few yards along the lane from Bryn-henllan to Pwllgwaelod.

DINAS ISLAND

Dinas is described as an island on the map and indeed it would take only a slight rise in sea level to cast it free. Cwm Dewi, the intervening channel, was gouged out by glacial meltwater to leave the steep sided wet valley we see today. The trees and marsh grasses provide a rich natural habitat for many small birds, more likely to be heard than seen. The wet, sheltered conditions encourage a succession of flowers throughout the year which in turn provide nectar attractive to butterflies.

You have a choice of onward routes to Cwm-yr-Eglwys; the path running through the valley is a justifiably attractive reason for avoiding the climb around the island, but then you would miss its spectacular northern cliffs. To avoid the disappointment of missing either experience, I suggest you do both, first tackling the headland.

Go past the car park and follow the track towards Island Farm. In a few metres/yards, after a cattle grid, leave the road as it bends right and take a path on the left (signposted Coast Path) to climb to the top of the headland. From there it is downhill, more or less steeply, but with an occasional climb to add variety (and also to give respite to those walking in the opposite direction). The path eventually joins a lane behind some cottages. Turn left towards the few houses and ruined church that make the village of Cwm-yr-Eglwys.

The climb is amply rewarded by the panorama from the top. Dinas projects from the land separating the bay of Fishguard behind from that of Newport ahead. Almost the whole of the coast from Strumble to Cemaes

Needle Rock from Dinas Head

Head is visible, and a pause on the summit provides an opportunity to reflect on your memories and anticipate the delights ahead, for although the end is now well in sight there are some surprises still to come. On the way down look for Needle Rock, a massive stack just off the cliffs. In spring and early summer it is crowded with herring gulls, shags and others competing for nest sites amongst its ledges and crevices. The cliffs below the path are home to fulmars and jackdaws, and the air is often full of birds exploiting the currents of air pushed up from below.

Cwm-yr-Eglwys at the eastern end of the valley benefits from the shelter given by Dinas Island, a fact that is demonstrated in the much more luxuriant vegetation that clothes the surrounding hillsides. This is small comfort to the ruins of the twelfth century church, dedicated to St Brynach, overlooking the beach. It was destroyed in October 1859 during a great storm. 120 years later, in 1979, another storm took away part of the graveyard.

The short walk through Cwm Dewi back to Pwllgwaelod is less strenuous. Turn right opposite the church and go through a small caravan site at the side of a car park, where a well constructed wheelchair path takes you the short distance through Cwm Dewi back to Pwllgwaelod, emerging beside a limekiln and a couple of buildings built low against the weather.

I forgot to point out when you first arrived here that one of the points of interest is the Sailor's Safety, an inn dating to 1593 and so named for the light it kept as a guide to shipping after dark.

Suitably refreshed, return to Cwm-yr-Eglwys.

Leave Cwm-yr-Eglwys turning left opposite the car park entrance into a lane climbing out of the village. After some 350 metres/yards a hedged grassy track (signposted Coast Path) leaves on the left. This leads back to the cliffs and so to the next bay at Aber Fforest. There, the path drops onto the beach. The onward path is signed across a field behind the beach (access a few metres/yards along a gravel drive running away from the beach), which then climbs back to the headland. A short cliff walk leads to Aber Rhigian, another quiet and sheltered bay.

Erosion at the eastern end of the cliffs above Aber Ysgol is causing the edges to crumble as the supporting rock falls away. Of further interest a few metres/yards on is a narrow chasm with sheer over-vertical sides plummeting downwards. By now you will have seen many examples of wave cut platforms, but those below these cliffs are the most extensive along the coast, and continue below the cliffs to the Nyfer estuary.

Cross the shingle at the head of Aber Rhigian, the onward path leaving over the bridge beyond. Climb a wooded bank to a grass covered slope. A pleasant walk above a series of inaccessible bays then takes you on to Parrog.

The vast expanse of the Nyfer estuary gradually reveals itself as the perspective changes. What at first appeared to be the head of a beach resolves into the Bennett, a huge sand bar that diverts the course of the Afon Nyfer from the northern bank to the rocks below the path on this side. The path meets the estuary at Careg Germain, where a small building above a slipway dated 1884 at one time housed the Newport lifeboat.

At Parrog the path drops to the shore in front of a row of houses, finally leaving it to pass a car park in front of Newport Boat Club. At high tide, an alternative is signed alongside a field behind the houses.

The vestiges of a quayside and the overgrown ruins of buildings at the side of the car park hint of Parrog's earlier importance as a port. By the sixteenth century it had developed as an important trade centre, dealing with other ports around the Irish Sea board and continental Europe. In the nineteenth century it was recognised for the ships that were built here. However, as with most of the ports we have passed, the industrial age and the railways took away the trade.

Pass the car park, just after which a well made path (signposted Coast Path) leaves the road to the left and heads upstream alongside the tidal marshes of the estuary. It ends about 1 kilometre (0.6 mile) on at the side of a road bridge crossing the Afon Nyfer.

Before crossing the bridge you must not miss Careg Coetan, a small but perfectly proportioned Neolithic dolmen just a few metres/yards away to the south-west. Turn right along the road, and then right again along a drive; it lies a few metres/yards up on the right.

Chapter Fifteen

NEWPORT to ST DOGMAEL'S

25.9 kilometres (16.1 miles)

The final leg of the journey follows the Afon Nyfer back to the sea before heading north-east along an almost unbroken line of towering cliffs that culminate dramatically in Cemaes Head. There, the coast turns in above the wide estuary of the Afon Teifi and the cliffs fall away to return you to the water's edge at St Dogmael's. There are a number of steep climbs along the way, but often, having achieved the height, you are compensated by long stretches of fairly level going with spectacular views in both directions. There are one or two places where high sheer cliffs close to the path may give a sense of exposure, and care needs to be exercised in wet or windy conditions. However, although strenuous it is an enjoyable walk and provides a fitting climax to the expedition.

Each section of the path has presented something new, and these few final kilometres will provide more than enough opportunity to divert you from your ultimate purpose.

The iron bridge across the Afon Nyfer was constructed in 1894. A medieval bridge on the site is supposed to have been demolished in the seventeenth century in an attempt to protect the town from plague. The stepping stones that served travellers during the intervening period can still be seen, sitting in the mud upstream. One can only marvel at the prodigious strides that the former inhabitants of the town must have been capable of in order to cross dry shod.

The estuary attracts many type of waders who come to feed in the mud revealed at low tide during the winter months. This in turn attracts bird watchers, who take advantage of the bridge's grandstand position (and the opportunity to remain in the comfort of their cars) to observe them. The locality is a wildfowl conservation area.

Cross the bridge, and follow a track (signposted Coast Path) downstream beside the river bank. It eventually turns away from the river to follow waymarks across a golf course (keep an eye open for flying golf balls), and eventually ends at a car park and café at the Bennett.

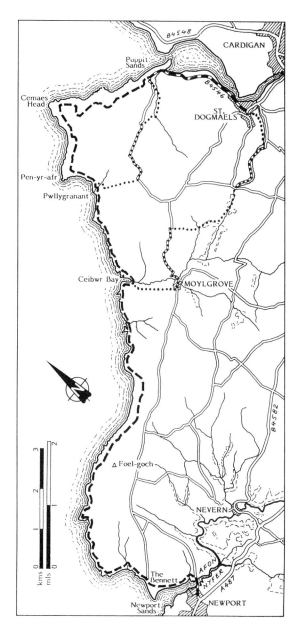

153

A couple of hundred metres from the bridge is a large limekiln, characteristically built close to the shore. The path gives a splendid view down the Nyfer, looking straight across to Dinas. Its huge mass rises from the land to face the sea; the separating valley of Cwm Dewi is clearly visible. The Bennett, to the left of the golf course, is a massive sand dune reaching across the mouth of the estuary, and diverting the course of the river to the opposite bank. The wind that created it is now in danger of destroying it. The effects of increasing numbers of feet are damaging the marram grass which holds it in place, and a conservation programme is under way to reconsolidate it. The dune is a natural coastal defence, and stabilisation coincidentally provides a much cheaper solution than the construction of artificial measures, which would otherwise become necessary to protect the estuary.

Cross the car park and leave over a stile on the opposite side (signposted Coast Path). The path undulates over low dunes behind the beach before climbing away from the estuary. Once back with the open sea it rises and falls, often quite steeply, following the lip of the cliffs. These stretch away into the distance, steadily getting higher until, on the flanks of Foel-goch, you are more than 150 metres (500 feet) above the sea. The path avoids some recent landslip in the region above Ogof Goch before losing height to the promontory fort at Castell Treruffydd.

The whole length of these airy cliffs provide an exhilarating walk with fine views in both directions. For long stretches the land falls away in ever steepening bracken covered slopes to bare rock faces far below. At intervals small bays have been gnawed out and are backed by bare cliffs of monumental proportions. As the path drops to Castell Treruffydd look back to the base of the cliffs, where there is a very fine arch. The outlines of the Iron Age fort marked on the map are difficult to discern. The surrounding cliffs are of crumbling shale and are much broken, their tops falling away, taking with them ever increasing portions of the promontory. The ground rises and falls in a most confused manner, but those with an imaginative eye will separate the ancient embankments from those which have been wrought by nature.

Beyond the tangle of hillocks and hullocks follow the path very steeply down to Traeth Bach and Pwll y Wrach. Part way down the path turns into the valley for an easier line of descent. The area has suffered recently from considerable erosion, so follow the signed deviations, both for your own safety and to allow the steep slopes to restabilise.

TRAETH BACH

I promised you more surprises and this is one of them. The steep path into the valley provides the best view of it and allows you to appreciate the sheer size of the appropriately named Pwll y Wrach, the Witches' Cauldron. It is a massive collapsed cave, open to the sea through a gigantic arch across which the path out of the valley climbs. Before continuing down the slope to explore it and the tiny bay in front, pause also to look back into the gully which is threatening to separate the small promontory from the land; it is most impressive.

The stream at the base of the valley passes through a small gorge, crossed by a concrete sleeper bridge. Apparently on its way directly to the beach, the stream disappears; investigation shows that it has broken through its bed and falls into a cave to flow to the right into Pwll y Wrach. The hole is so vast that a shingle bar has been thrown up by the waves crashing in through the open arch and there is a small beach in front of it. The bar holds back a small pool, behind which the walls of the crater rise up almost 60 metres (200 feet).

A tiny rocky bay looking out to meet the waves, the place is a wonderful spot, excavated out of horizontal beds of slate which have been polished smooth by the action of the waves. The sides of the cove are deeply undercut and several caves and hollows have been formed.

The path out is steep but quickly gains the necessary height to take you across the intervening headland to Ceibwr Bay. Just above a huge stack, Careg Wylan, the path joins the coast road. Turn left (signposted Coast Path) and follow it some 250 metres/yards to Ceibwr or alternatively leave again a few metres/yards further on, and walk above the rocks at the mouth of the bay.

Ceibwr is a narrow glacial outflow channel, fed now by two streams flowing from the delightfully wooded valleys of Cwm Trewyddel and Cwm Tawel, whose confluence is a few metres/yards upstream. The pebble beach is dominated by a steep slope to the east up which, inevitably, the onward path lies.

Go down to the beach where a sturdy slate bridge leads across a lively stream. Walk around the head of the bay and leave up a steep track (signposted Coast Path) towards Pen Castell.

The Iron Age fort to which the name of Pen Castell refers lies below the path and is not obvious. There is no access.

The path passes the landward side of the house before reverting to the very edge of the cliffs. It then becomes less exposed and

makes its way north-eastwards over the flanks of Foel Hendre to Pwllygranant. There are a number of sections on this stretch of the route where the path was completely washed out by the heavy rains of the 1993 storms, particularly where it is crossed by drainage gullies. The path had to be closed for a time but repairs have now been completed and a couple of new footbridges have been constructed to take the path over their now exaggerated clefts.

The descent to the stream at Pwllygranant is steep, and the path zigzags up the valley to lessen the gradient. At the bottom a bridge crosses a stream, which continues down the valley, before disappearing over a small waterfall onto the beach. The path which followed it down has been washed away.

PWLLYGRANANT

Along the Coast Path the hillsides around Pwllygranant suffered most from the storm which hit the Welsh coast during the night of 12-13 June 1993. Considerable disruption and damage to property and the countryside occurred in many areas as far north as Colwyn Bay, mainly as a result of torrential rainfall. The area around Cardigan suffered as much as anywhere, with a reported 118 millimetres (4.6 inches) of rain falling within the 24-hour period. The banks of water courses and valleys, unable to contain the torrents of water thundering through them, were ripped away, mature trees being carried off by the tremendous undercutting power of the water. In other places the sheer quantity of water washed away whole areas of landslip. It was a terrifying event for those who helplessly witnessed its impartial and single-minded ferocity.

Damage to the Coast Path was concentrated in the valleys behind Traeth Bâch, Ceibwr Bay and Pwllygranant and sections of the cliff path, particularly the segment just walked, Ceibwr Bay to Pwllygranant. Shallow stream beds were transformed into miniature gorges, and sections of path washed away, leaving gaping abysses. However by the end of summer 1993 many of the scars on the valley sides were becoming covered with new greenery as the surrounding vegetation seized the opportunity of an open space. National Park rangers have now repaired the damage and the natural healing processes of nature are already concealing its effects. In time this will help to stabilise the fragile slopes. You can assist the process by following only the marked paths.

The valley behind Pwllygranant is a wild and lonely place, the havoc

Erosion above
Traeth Godir-côch

created by the storm enhancing its apparent isolation. The beach is narrow and rocky, and access to it requires a scramble.

The onward route (signposted Coast Path) is up a stepped path on the opposite side of the valley, it is quite steep in places. Once on top of the cliff it undulates more sympathetically upwards, emulating the gentle folds in the exposed bedding of the cliffs. There is more climbing as you turn away from Traeth y Rhedyn to reach the highest point along the whole walk above Traeth Godir-côch, at over 175 metres (almost 575 feet).

There is a breathtaking retrospective view as you leave the valley, that competes for your attention with the complex and beautiful patterns displayed in the intricate layering and folding of Pen-yr-Afr ahead. You may well feel that some of the finest panoramas have been saved for the final kilometres of the walk.

CEMAES HEAD

Once the top of the cliff has been gained the gradient becomes generally easier apart from an occasional dip and pull to keep your interest. The cliffs below alternate between steep grassy slopes and sheer vertical faces, sometimes running alongside the path, and providing excellent dramatic views along the coast on a clear day. Behind is Strumble Head, its lighthouse blinking its message from the point. The mass of Garn Fawr rises impressively to its left and, before it, the open mouth of Fishguard Bay and Dinas Head. To the north-east, the cliffs behind Traeth y Rhedyn rise 120 metres (400 feet) from the sea, the complex folding that created them becoming more distinct as you approach.

As you approach the crest it is perhaps time for reflection, to savour the memories of the places passed and take an occasional glance back to ascertain the point at which their tangibility disappeared.

Over the crest the path gently loses height towards Cemaes Head, where it leaves the cliff edge and turns in towards the Teifi estuary. A field path eventually becomes a grass track down to the farm at Allt-y-goed.

As you descend, the wild and rugged beauty behind is exchanged for the more gentle slopes that contain the Afon Teifi. Your final glimpse of that vast northern sweep of cliffs comes just before you turn your back on Cemaes Head to walk up the Teifi Valley. Cardigan Island and the coast beyond come into view. The sight no longer represents a challenge for the following day, nor generates anticipation for what is to come. Nevertheless the view is not without charm. The Teifi winds from side to side as if contemplating the best line of attack on the sand bar that all but blocks its freedom to the sea. At low tide vast sandy beaches stretch back along its banks.

The Teifi is a salmon river, and the monks who settled at the abbey in St Dogmael's are said to have fished for them, introducing the now traditional coracles and seine nets still used here.

Allt-y-goed lies in a valley and the way onwards lies along the farm track, climbing out on the opposite side. The track becomes a pleasant lane which steadily drops for the next 2.3 kilometres (1.4 miles) to the lifeboat station and car park at Poppit Sands.

Set into the wall outside the cafe opposite the lifeboat station are two plaques, identical to those that witnessed the start of your journey at Amroth. However the Coast Path does not end until it reaches St Dogmael's, a further 2 kilometres (1.25 miles) up the river.

The natural boundary between the old counties of Pembrokeshire and Cardiganshire was the Afon Teifi. However the administrative boundary crossed the river, putting the areas immediately to the north and south of St Dogmael's into Cardiganshire, but leaving St Dogmael's with Pembrokeshire, reflecting the ancient landholding of the Lords of Ceredigion and St Dogmael's Abbey. The last 2 kilometres (1.25 miles) of the walk therefore lie within the old county of Cardigan, although you will actually be back in Pembrokeshire when you finish the walk.

Follow the road upstream beyond the car park to St Dogmael's. It leaves the river bank for a short distance but returns to the water at the northern boundary of the village beside a slipway. You have returned to Pembrokeshire and reached the end of the walk.

ST DOGMAEL'S

St Dogmael's is not without interest and provides some opportunity for exploration before setting off home. The village takes its name from St Dogfael, a Celtic monk descended from one of the local princes. He founded a cell here in the fifth or sixth century, and his influence spread as far as Brittany. His community here was later sacked by Norse raiders.

At the beginning of the twelfth century Robert Fitz-Martin, the Norman first Lord of Cemaes, established an abbey close to the original Welsh community at the foot of Cwm Degwell above the river. It was a Benedictine foundation of the order of Tiron in France. The same order established two other houses in Pembrokeshire with the same patronage as this; one, you will remember, was on Caldey. The other, Pill Priory, was just to the north of Milford Haven. St Dogmael's Abbey, as that at Pill, is now a picturesque ruin. It has for company the Victorian parish church of St Thomas, which was built alongside it in 1847. Inside the church is the Sagranus Stone, which in 1848 performed a similar service in the decipherment of Ogham, an ancient Irish 20 character alphabet, to that which the Rosetta Stone played in the understanding of Egyptian hieroglyphics. An inscription dating from the fifth or sixth century and translated as "The stone of Sagranus, son of Cunotamus" was found to be carved both in Latin and Ogham script.

You have returned almost to the meridian from which you started, a mere 40 kilometres (24.8 miles) north of Amroth. It has more than likely taken you some two weeks to do it and your feet will have travelled eight times that distance; so much for following signposts! If you are returning to Amroth for your car, you had better take out your compass and set it due south.

Chapter Sixteen
CIRCULAR WALKS

The coast does not hold a monopoly of the area's footpaths and there are many other paths, tracks and quiet lanes worthy of exploration. A number conveniently link stretches of the coast, and make them ideal for incorporation into a circular walk. I have found a small number of paths marked on the OS maps to have fallen into disuse, and suggest here only routes that are both easily passable and maintain accepted rights of way. Therefore occasionally lanes have been used rather than a more direct or otherwise preferable field path. My routes are merely suggestions to whet your appetite, and encourage you to continue your exploration in other areas of the National Park. All the walks are based upon completing some section of the Coast Path and do not venture into the other major areas of the National Park, the Mynydd Preseli, Cwm Gwuan and the higher reaches of the Daugleddau, which are beyond the scope of this guide. Route descriptions refer to the inland sections of the walk, the coastal section being contained within the main text.

AMROTH AND WISEMAN'S BRIDGE - 7 kilometres (4.5 miles)

Sheltered from the worst of the prevailing weather, this part of the coast is rich in vegetation, particularly in the several deep valleys that reach into the hinterland. This first walk follows a short stretch of high cliff and returns along two such valleys, both thickly wooded and typical of the botanical variety that the coastal strip displays. They were extensively mined for iron ore and anthracite during the last century but only scant evidence of the former industry now remains. In Pleasant Valley behind Wiseman's Beach the path follows the line of a mineral railway that connected Stepaside with Saundersfoot, and on the Colby Estate north of Amroth some of the old workings can be found in the trees.

The Colby Estate is now owned by the National Trust, and although the house, designed by Nash and built in 1903, is not open to view you can visit its woodland gardens. They were laid out at the

Carn Ogof to Dinas Mawr
Pwll Deri from Dinas Mawr

Pwll Hes'cwm
River Teifi to Cardigan Island

end of the last century and extend along the valley on either side of the footpath. In spring and early summer daffodils, rhododendrons, azaleas and bluebells provide a veritable feast of colour. Also not to be missed is the walled garden, privately maintained by the present residents of Colby. It rises above the house and contains, in addition to a wonderful array of plants, a charming gazebo, designed in the mid seventies by a local architect, Wyn Jones. The splendid interior of the pavilion has been cleverly painted by an American artist (note the reference to Abraham Lincoln on the scrap of paper deceivingly pinned on the back wall) to produce a striking *trompe l'oeil* effect.

There is car parking at both Amroth (SN 161 070) and Wiseman's Bridge (SN 145 061). The walk is described from Amroth.

Join the Coast Path at the western end of Amroth village and walk to Wiseman's Bridge. Just before the Coast Path leaves the road at the far end of the beach take a track on the right, which follows the stream up Pleasant Valley. Eventually it crosses the stream and then ends at a road opposite Mill House. Turn left and walk a short distance to Mill House Caravan Park. Turn right into the campsite and cross to a signed footpath on the opposite side of the field. This leads over a stile and into a meadow. Go half left, climbing up to a gap in the top wall by a small garage; continue past it to the lane beyond.

Turn right and follow it down to a sharp right bend. Leave the road for the track ahead and continue past the houses. After the last house take a marked footpath on the right which leads to a gorse and shrub covered hillside. Climb the hill on a diagonal line to the right to find a field gate and stile at the top. Cross into the field (waymarked) and walk ahead along the left boundary. At the top corner cross another waymarked stile to join a hedged grass path. Continue to walk ahead, eventually passing Cwmrath Farm, where you then follow its access track to the road just north of Summerhill. Turn right and then immediately left to follow a bridleway to Skerry Back. A waymarked path continues past the house into the woodland beyond. The path then drops quite steeply, eventually emerging onto a drive beside Colby House. Follow the drive to its end and turn right onto the road.

Walk past the house and turn right again at the entrance to the woodland garden (signposted Footpath). Continue past the café and reception (where tickets to visit the gardens can be purchased) and follow the drive down the wooded valley. Beyond the wood the drive ends at a road, which you then follow down to the sea front at Amroth. The car park from which you started lies a short distance to the right.

STACKPOLE AND BOSHERSTON LILY PONDS -
10.3 kilometres (6.4 miles)

A delightful walk along an impressive stretch of limestone cliffs passing a number of incredible caves, blowholes and stacks and two fine sandy beaches, Barafundle and Broad Haven. The return route leaves the coast over a developing dune system to follow the longest of Bosherston's lily ponds towards Stackpole village. A walk along quiet country lanes returns you to the coast. Delightful at any time of year, the mass of flowering lilies that carpet the lakes in early summer add an extra bonus to the woodland that surround them. There is a car park at Stackpole Quay (SR 991 958).

From the car park at Stackpole join the Coast Path and follow it to the head of the beach at Broad Haven. There, walk away from the

Bosherston Lily Ponds

shore along the right-hand bank of the lake to cross a bridge over the base of the northern reach of water. Turn right and continue beside the water, now on the left bank. At the top end of the lake the path climbs from its shore up a grand staircase to the site of the now demolished Stackpole Court; only the converted stable block now remains. Join the drive running from it and continue out of the park to the road. Turn right and walk up to and through the village. Where the road divides on its far side choose the right fork towards Freshwater East. A short distance beyond, turn right again down a narrow lane to return to the car park at Stackpole Quay.

ANGLE PENINSULA - 14 kilometres (8.7 miles)

The geographical structure of the Angle peninsula, like those of Dale and Marloes to the west and Dinas Island to the north, maximises the amount of Coast Path covered in relation to return passage, and provides ideal introductions to Coast Path walking. Like many of the circular walks suggested, this is one of contrasts. Rugged sandstone cliffs cut by a number of drainage valleys on the southern section provide an energetic walk, well representative of many sections of the path. There is much to see in the erosive incursions that the sea has made into the cliffs below. Wooded slopes line the more regular cliffs of the northern edge before they are interrupted by the kidney shaped indentation of Angle Bay. At low tide the bay is a wide expanse of sheltered muddy beach that encourages a variety of feeding birds. There are three convenient car parks, at West Angle Bay (SM 854 032), in the village of Angle (SM 866 028) and at Freshwater West (SM 885 003). The walk is described from West Angle Bay.

The coast path leaves above the northern corner of the beach and is followed to Angle village and then beyond along a tarmac drive at the back of Angle Bay. Remain with the drive where the coast path abandons it for the beach, and follow it as it turns inland, climbing through Bangeston Wood to meet the road. There turn left and walk for about 350 metres/yards. Leave by a signed footpath through a gate on the right. Walk ahead, following the right boundary of the field, continuing in the same direction across the subsequent field, finally dropping into a shallow valley overgrown with bracken. Walk directly across it and, reaching the field margin on the opposite side, turn right to head for the coast above Gravel Bay, where a stile returns you to the Coast Path. West Angle Bay is to the right.

DALE PENINSULA - 10.2 kilometres (6.3 miles)

Directly opposite the Angle peninsula is St Ann's Head, the southernmost tip of the Dale peninsula. In outline, vaguely reminiscent of some distorted animal's paw, it faces the inlet to Milford Haven, with its "claws", a succession of four minor promontories, guarding the approach. Indeed, such was their command over the entrance to the estuary that two of them were fortified during the nineteenth century. Virtually the whole of the walk follows the coast, there being only a short return across the narrow neck of the peninsula behind the village of Dale. It is an easy, pleasurable walk. There is a car park opposite the beach in the village (SM 811 058).

Leave the village along the coast road, climbing a narrow wooded lane towards Dale Fort. The path leaves the road on the right just before it reaches the fort. Continue around the coast to Westdale Bay where a signed footpath to the right leads across the intervening meadow to Dale Castle. A short farm track leads to the road, from where it is only a short walk back to the village ahead.

MARLOES PENINSULA - 14.2 kilometres (8.8 miles)

Hard volcanic rocks underlie the northern half of the Marloes peninsula, and manifestly contrast with the sedimentary strata that compose its southern aspect. The dissimilarity is heightened by their relationship to the prevailing winds; the north, being more sheltered, is clothed more luxuriously in vegetation. A good and relatively level path exists around the coast. My suggestion takes in the whole of the peninsula, but shorter walks are made possible along footpaths meeting the coast above Watery Bay and towards the western end of Marloes Sands on the southern side. Both return to the road west of Marloes Court Farm, opposite which a footpath leads in a north-easterly direction through a field to the suggested starting point. There is car parking beside the road at (SM 786 085), west of Marloes village, and also at Martin's Haven (SM 760 089) and near Runwayskiln youth hostel (SM 779 082).

From the layby west of Marloes village, walk back along the road to the village clock tower. Turn right along a path beside the Foxes' Inn to cut across to the Runwayskiln road, almost opposite its junction with a farm lane. Follow that lane south to the farm at Little Marloes. Immediately before reaching the farm take a signed footpath which continues ahead along the right-hand boundary of a field. Maintain the same direction across the fields to reach the edge of the wartime Dale Airfield. There, turn right and follow its perimeter runway south and then east, passing The Hookses, once a small farm in prewar days. A short distance beyond, a tarmac track (signed Footpath) leaves to the right. Follow this to a gate where a further sign directs you right, across a small field to the coast above Westdale Bay. Turn right onto the Coast Path. Follow it round the peninsula to Musselwick Sands. Above the bay turn right onto a path coming steeply up from the beach. It leads across the field to emerge on the road opposite the start point.

The vast concave sweep of St Bride's Bay provides no opportunity for shortened inland returns. That should not deter you, however, from walking sections of the fine coastline and either retracing your steps or making use of the extensive, albeit non too frequent, public transport service. I would suggest, though, that you used such conveniences for your outward trip rather than rely on them at the end of the day.

RAMSEY SOUND - 9.2 kilometres (5.7 miles)

An easy walk along a good path that provides some of the most attractive coastal scenery of the whole Coast Path. Although facing directly to the open sea, this south-western tip of the St David's peninsula receives some protection from the island of Ramsey, just a short distance across the Sound. Particularly in spring, the abundance of wild flowers along the old field banks add a special delight. The walk can be undertaken either from Porthstinian (SM 724 252) or Porth Clais (SM 741 242); there is convenient parking at both places. The walk is described from Porth Clais.

The car park lies behind Porth Clais inlet, a drowned glacial outflow valley, now flooded to create an attractive and well sheltered harbour. Walk down the western side of the valley, the path leaving the harbour by the limekilns to gain the sea cliffs. A meandering path leads to Porthstinian.

Leave the path and walk up the lane away from the coast for 1 kilometre (0.6 mile) to a junction. There turn right and walk on, past Clegyr-Boia on the left, a defended settlement where artifacts dating from Neolithic times have been discovered, and return to the coast at Porth Clais.

ST DAVID'S HEAD - 5 kilometres (3 miles)

Involving some uphill sections, although not too steep and on good ground, the walk along St David's Head provides magnificent views over spectacular cliffs and passes a fine example of an Iron Age fortified settlement and a Neolithic dolmen. For those with energy to spare, the ascent of Carn Llidi is well rewarded by the panorama from its summit. There is a large car park at Porth Mawr (SM 734 271).

Join the Coast Path to the north of the car park beside a telephone box and climb onto St David's Head. Follow the high ground in a north-easterly direction, but as it loses height towards the far end, head to the right to pick up a clear path returning by the far side of Carn Llidi. Follow it around the southern flank, going past the path down to the youth hostel on the left. A little further on, again on the left, is a rough track which returns down the hill, meeting the road just east of the car park. If you wish to climb to the top of Carn Llidi continue a little beyond the descending track, where a path on the right climbs to the top.

TRAETH LLYFN, PORTH-GAIN AND ABER DRAW - 8 kilometres (5 miles)

The coastline either side of Porth-gain has been much exploited in the past for its stone, slate and china clay, but time has healed many of the wounds and the now deserted workings have been softened by the passage of time. Their remains are not without interest and compete for your attention with the coastal erosion of the relatively soft shales and slates.

There is parking at both Porth-gain (SM 814 325) and on Ynys Barry above Traeth Llyfn (SM 803 319), access being along a track running through Barry Island Farm, leaving the Llanrhian to Porth-gain road about halfway between the two hamlets. Opportunities to park at Aber Draw are limited, and it is better to leave cars in Trefin, a little further to the east. The walk is described from Traeth Llyfn.

The Coast Path passes the end of the car park above the beach; turn right and follow it along the cliff tops, passing Porth-gain to the road at Swyn-y-Don Farm. The terrain throughout is gentle, although there is a steep descent down steps into Porth-gain; the climb away on the other side is less severe. Turn left at Swyn-y-Don to go down to the beach at Aber Draw, 250 metres/yards further on. Then retrace your steps to the farm and carry on up the hill towards Llanrhian. About 450 metres/yards beyond Swyn-y-Don climb a waymarked stile into a field on the right. Walk diagonally left across the field to a gate on its far side. Go through that and continue to walk ahead, following the left field boundary; the path becomes a track at the next field gate that leads to a farm at Henllys.

Continue past the farm, climbing a gravel track below Felindre House. Just after the track bends sharply left, cross a stile into a field on the right and walk diagonally left to a stile in its far corner. Continue in the same direction across the next field to emerge on the Porth-gain - Llanrhian road almost opposite the entrance to Barry Farm. Cross over and walk along the track, continuing past the farmhouse (now a hotel) and out-buildings. About 0.5 kilometre (0.3 mile) further on, the track drops down the field to the right to the car park above Traeth Llyfn.

ABER CASTLE AND ABER MAWR - 8 kilometres (5 miles)

A fine walk along a rocky coast that has been much eroded into a succession of tiny bays. The terrain is fairly easy, with only one steep drop and re-climb as the path negotiates a stream flowing to the sea at Pwllstrodur. The climbs out of Aber Castle and Aber Mawr are less steep. If you wish to make the walk a little longer Aber Bach is only a short distance beyond Aber Mawr, and both bays are backed by delightfully wooded valleys, each served by good footpaths. The walk can be shortened by leaving the coast at Pwllstrodur. There is parking at both Aber Castle (SM 853 336) and above Aber Mawr (SM 883 347).

Leave Aber Castle by the Coast Path above the northern side of the bay to gain the cliffs. The path meets the shore at Pwllstrodur and

climbs again over Mynydd Morfa before dropping to Aber Mawr. To return to Aber Castle, retrace your steps a short distance along the Coast Path, climbing away from the beach. By the first stile, two paths are signed to the left; sharp left heads up the valley behind Aber Mawr through Pen-y-allt Wood to the road about 0.75 kilometre (0.5 mile) away. However the return follows the second, a grass bridle track. It leads over Mynydd Morfa before dropping into the valley behind Pwllstrodur, where it is often muddy. Follow its continuation to emerge at the side of a house, Carnachen-wyd. There turn right onto a tarmac lane; about 200 metres/yards along the lane, a signed footpath comes across the field on the right from Pwllstrodur. At the end of the lane turn right and follow the road back to Aber Castle, 1 kilometre (0.6 mile) away.

PWLL DERI TO HARBOUR VILLAGE (GOODWICK), RETURNING OVER GARN FAWR - 19.5 kilometres (12 miles)

There is parking at both Pwll Deri (SM 893 385) and at Harbour village (SM 948 391), although be careful not to obstruct the bus turning area. Strumble Head has a rugged coastline, continually twisting and turning around innumerable small bays and headlands. The cliffs are regularly split by streams and therefore the path regularly falls and climbs between the cliff tops and the sea. Although presented as a single walk, the coast can be left at Strumble Lighthouse (SM 897 413), Porthsychan (SM 905 407), Penrhyn (SM 913 407), Carregwastad (SM 925 403) or Cwm Felin (SM 925 400) to make shorter walks.

In early autumn, many of the bays around the coast are turned into seal nurseries, and the plaintive cries of the pups echoing from the cliff walls at times sound almost human. The route returns by crossing the summit of Garn Fawr from the east, a less arduous ascent than from Pwll Deri; on a clear day there are magnificent views in all directions.

Join the coast path by the youth hostel at Pwll Deri and follow it to Harbour Village above Goodwick. At the southern end of the street through Harbour village, turn sharp right along a farm track to Penrhiw Farm. Carry on through the yard, leaving by a gate at the far side, opposite which a grass track leads away from the farm. The track turns first right and then left, skirting a house, Anfield, eventually ending at a road junction. Take the lane opposite, signed Llanwnda, and walk to Llanwnda Farm. Pass beyond the farm buildings and immediately take a track on the left, designated ANADDAS I FODUR - UNSUITABLE FOR MOTORS. Take the right fork as it divides a short distance further on, dropping to Pont Eglwys before climbing to eventually meet the road. There turn right and walk past Tre-Howel until a grass track leaves on the left (signed Footpath) towards a cottage marked on the map as the North Pole! Just before the cottage bear right on a grass path that continues up the gorse covered hillside, eventually following a low field wall on the right to end at a grass track. Turn right and walk down to its junction with the road from Strumble Head.

Turn left, climbing towards Garn Fawr. As the road crests the hill there is a small car park on the right. At the back of this a signed footpath climbs to the top of Garn Fawr and then drops down on its opposite flank, passing through Tal-y-gaer Farm to join the road opposite Pwll Deri youth hostel and the Coast Path. The car park at Pwll Deri lies a few metres/yards down the road to the left.

CIRCUMAMBULATION OF DINAS ISLAND -
4.5 kilometres (2.8 miles)

A short walk, but not to be underestimated, the climb to the top of the head is taxing from either direction. Once there, however, the effort is repaid by extensive views along the coast in both directions. The eastern cliffs of the island around Needle Rock are rewarding for the number of seabirds that nest on the rocks. There is parking at both Pwll Gwaelod (SM 005 399) and Cwm-yr-Eglwys (SM 014 399). The route is described in the main text.

CEIBWR BAY, PWLLYGRANANT, CEMAES HEAD, POPPIT SANDS AND ST DOGMAEL'S - 19.8 kilometres (12.3 miles)

This is both a long and strenuous walk, but on a fine day is a rewarding excursion, combining a high rugged cliff walk with a delightful stroll (albeit partly along the road) through the impressive valley of Cwm Degwel and across to the village of Moylgrove. Serious storm erosion and overgrown paths unfortunately preclude a more direct cross-country route.

Although described as starting from Poppit, personal preference will determine whether you elect to undertake the road walk through St Dogmael's at the beginning or the end of the day and, of course, in which direction you walk. If you have two cars and choose to avoid the cross-country section, I would still recommend that you round off the day with a stroll through the delightful valley of Cwm Degwel. There is a car park at Poppit Sands (SN 152 485), by permission from the farm at Allt-y-goed (SN 135 494), and roadside parking at St Dogmael's (SN 162 458) and Ceibwr Bay (SN 108 457).

Follow the B4546 from the car park at Poppit Sands into St Dogmael's village. There, turn right to climb steeply before turning left into Cwm, part way up the hill. Go to its end, where a signed footpath leaves on the left, climbing above the abbey. The path gives splendid views across the wooded precipitous slopes that enclose Cwm Degwel. Eventually it falls behind some cottages to join a quiet lane running along the base of the valley. There, turn right and follow it to a junction at the head of the valley.

Cross over and continue ahead along a wooded farm track towards Pantsaeson Farm. After about 1 kilometre (0.6 mile) at a junction, turn right, eventually coming to a gate at a second junction. Continue through the gate (waymarked) to the track's end, where a gate leads to a small field bounded on the left by a stable block. Cross to its opposite corner, where a track leads on past some out-buildings on the left. Just beyond, turn right (again waymarked) through another gate, immediately before a high wall. Follow this track which eventually ends at a road at Gilfach.

Turn left and follow the road for 2 kilometres (1.3 miles) down to Moylgrove. At the bottom of the hill bear right into the village and then immediately turn right again to Ceibwr Bay, 1.5 kilometres (0.9 mile) down the lane. There, the Coast Path leaves the road on the right just before the beach. Follow the Coast Path to Pwllgranant and then around Cemaes Head to Allt-y-goed and finally to Poppit.

PWLLYGRANANT AND CEMAES HEAD FROM POPPIT SANDS - 10.2 kilometres (6.4 miles)

This is a somewhat shorter version of the previous walk, but remains nonetheless a demanding walk. It crosses Cemaes Head along the line of two valleys that approach each other from opposite coasts, which almost, but not quite, connect, thus involving inevitable climb and descent. Pwllygranant is an isolated valley breaking through the highest cliffs encountered along the Coast Path, out of which there is a steep climb to the cliffs above Traeth Godir-côch and on to Cemaes Head. The return is along field paths and a narrow lane above the mouth of the Afon Teifi to Poppit Sands. There is a car park at Poppit Sands (SN 152 485) and by permission from the farm at Allt-y-goed (SN 135 494).

Leave the car park along the B4546 heading west away from the beach. After some 300 metres/yards, take a drive on the left into Cardigan Bay Leisure Park. Continue past the site offices and swimming pool towards two cottages, Old Millers Cottage and Manian Mill. Between them is a farm gate (signposted Footpath) to a grass track following a stream to another gate, through which turn right, again following the line of the stream.

After a short distance the way ahead is barred by a gate. There, turn right and follow the fence line back to the stream, where it can be crossed to reach a field on the opposite bank. Climb up along its left boundary to a gate at the top and go left through it into the adjacent field. Walk ahead following the top boundary, and leave by a stile, hidden in the hedge on the right, immediately past the farm buildings, marked Trecwyn Isaf on the map.

Over the stile turn left along a hedged track, taking a right fork to return you to the road. There, turn left and follow it for about 1.5 kilometres (0.9 mile) as it climbs upwards above Cwm yr Esgyr. At the top, immediately after it bends sharply to the left, take a farm track on the right to Granant-isaf. Walk on through the farmyard, leaving through two successive gates (signposted Footpath) to a rough track dropping towards a cottage identified as Graig. Before reaching the cottage, cross a stile on the left (signposted Footpath). Go ahead along the right field boundary to another stile. Cross this and again follow the right boundary around to cross yet another stile, diagonally ahead. The path then falls, roughly along the line of a stream, into a gully at the head of Pwllygranant. The final section is steep, dropping to the bottom of a waterfall below Gernos. Cross this second stream and follow it to the coast and the Coast Path. Turn right, and follow it around Cemaes Head, eventually returning to Poppit Sands.

APPENDICES

ACCOMMODATION GUIDE

The Accommodation Guide is based on information provided by proprietors. The facilities offered and opening periods may change from time to time. Although not listed, some proprietors have expressed a willingness to provide car parking facilities or end of day transport and may also accept advance postal packages or (particularly campsites and farms) sell basic provisions. Walkers should confirm directly with each establishment in advance what they can offer and the current charge.

The list has been produced in order of progression around the coast from south to north in order to assist both day and long distance walkers in planning their itinerary. Only establishments on or close to the coast have been included and the list is neither exhaustive, nor does it imply a classification of standard or quality. Grid references are approximate. Youth hostels are often closed for part of the day, opening for visitors during the later part of the afternoon. They may not be open on all days of the week, particularly at the beginning and end of the season. Intending visitors should check details with the current YHA Guide.

Walkers, or indeed proprietors, with additional information or comment for inclusion in future editions should contact the author via the publisher.

KEY TO CHARTS

Acc	-	Accommodation	S	-	Shower
EM	-	Evening meal	T	-	Toilet
PL	-	Packed lunch	DF	-	Drying facilities
V	-	Vegetarian	Pr H	-	Private house
F	-	Flasks	G H	-	Guest house
NS	-	Non-smoking	Y H	-	Youth Hostel
D	-	Dogs	Camp	-	Camp site
S/B	-	Shower/bath	Hol	-	Holiday site
E	-	Ensuite			

ACCOMMODATION LIST

Name and Address	Telephone	Open	Grid Ref	Acc	EM	PL	V	F	NS	D	S/B	E	Camp	S	T	DF
Lynne & Valerie Evans Beach Haven Amroth Narberth SA67 8NG	01834 813310	III to XI	SN 164070	G H	-	-	✓	✓	-	✓	✓	-				
Mr & Mrs R. Williamson Ashdale Guest House Amroth Narberth SA67 8NA	01834 813853	I to XII	SN 161071	G H	✓	✓	✓	✓	-	-	✓	-				
Mrs Gwen Grecian Pinewood Cliff Road Wiseman's Bridge Narberth SA67 8NU	01834 811082	I to XII	SN 149065	Pr H	-	✓	-	✓	-	-	✓	✓				
Mrs M. Kemble Wiseman's Bridge Inn Wiseman's Bridge Saundersfoot SA69 9AU	01834 813236	III to I	SN 147062	Inn & Camp	✓	✓	✓	✓	✓	✓	✓	-	hol	✓	✓	-
Mrs G.I. Hope Cliff House Wogan Ter. Saundersfoot SA69 9HA	01834 813931	I to XII	SN 136049	Hotel	✓	-	✓	✓	-	✓	✓	✓				
Malcolm & Jennifer Quinn Primrose Cottage Stammer Rd Saundersfoot SA69 9HH	01834 811080	I to XII	SN 136046	Pr H	-	✓	✓	✓	✓	✓	✓	✓				
F.P. & A.R. Williams Jalna Hotel Stammers Road Saundersfoot SA69 9HH	01834 812282	III to X	SN 135046	Hotel	✓	✓	✓	✓	-	✓	✓	✓				

173

Name and Address	Telephone	Open	Grid Ref	Acc	EM	PL	V	F	NS	D	S/B	E	Camp	S	T	DF
Mr & Mrs Gordon Booth Pen-Fro The Glen Saundersfoot SA69 9NT	01834 812445	I to XII	SN 137044	Pr H	-	✓	-	✓	✓	✓	✓	-				✓
Mr Dennis Reed Trevayne Farm New Hedges Saundersfoot SA69 9DL	01834 813402	IV to X	SN 142032	Camp	-	-	-	-	-	-	-	-	hol	✓	✓	✓
Mr A John Meadow Farm Northcliff Tenby SA70 8AU	01834 844829	IV to X	SN 133015	Camp	-	-	-	-	-	-	-	*	basic	✓	✓	-
Mrs E Peachey Bartlett House 15 The Norton Tenby SA70 8AA	01834 842600	IV to X	SN 133008	Pr H	✓	✓	-	✓	-	✓	✓	-				
Mr & Mrs G Hughes Glenthorne Guest House 9 Deer Park Tenby SA70 7LE	01834 842300	I to XII	SN 131006	G H	✓	✓	✓	✓	-	✓	✓	✓				
Mrs P Percival Lyndale Guest House Warren Street Tenby SA70 7JX	01834 842836	I to XII	SN 130005	G H	-	-	✓	-	✓	✓	✓	-				
Mrs Cormack Ivy Bank Guest House Harding Street Tenby SA70 7LL	01834 842311	I to XII	SN 131006	G H	✓	-	✓	✓	✓	-	✓	✓				
Mr P Dickenson Caldey View Guest House St Julian's Street Tenby SA70 7BD	01834 842126	III to X	SN 136004	G H	-	-	✓	✓	✓	✓	✓	✓				
Mr L Watts Crossing Cottage Penally Tenby SA70 7PP	01834 842291	I to XII	SS 122996	Pr H	-	-	-	✓	-	-	✓	-				

Name and Address	Telephone	Open	Grid Ref	Acc	EM	PL	V	F	NS	D	S/B	E	Camp	S	T	DF
Mrs M Penn Myrtle House Penally Tenby SA70 7PU	01834 843623	I to XII	SS 118992	Pr H	-	-	✓	✓	✓	✓	✓	-				
Mrs L Nightingale Brambles Lodge Penally Tenby SA70 7QE	01834 842393	III to X	SS 112989	G H	✓	✓	✓	✓	-	✓	✓	✓				
Mrs M Boot Lydstep Home Farm Lydstep SA70 7SG	01834 871208	I to XII	SS 087983	Farm & Camp	-	-	✓	✓	-	-	✓	-	basic	-	-	-
Manorbier Youth Hostel Manorbier SA70 7TT	01834 871803	III to X	SS 081975	Y H	✓	-	✓	✓	-	-	✓	-	basic	✓	✓	-
Mrs J Bell Hillgarth Manorbier Near Tenby SA70 7TN	01834 871266	I to XII	SS 077981	G H	-	-	✓	✓	✓	-	✓	✓				
Mrs D Jordan The Dak Manorbier SA70 8QR	01834 871209	IV to VIII	SS 058977	Pr H	-	✓	-	✓	✓	✓	-	✓				
Miss B Phillips Seahorses Freshwater East Lamphey SA71 5LA	01646 672405	V to IX	SS 017984	Pr H	-	-	✓	✓	-	-	✓	-				
Mr R Ireland East Trewent Farm Freshwater East Lamphey SA71 5LR	01646 672127	I to XII	SS 009973	Farm	✓	✓	✓	✓	-	✓	✓	-				
Mr & Mrs A Webster St Govan's Inn Bosherston Pembroke SA71 5DN	01646 661311	I to XII	SR 966947	Inn	✓	✓	✓	✓	✓	-	✓	✓				

Name and Address	Telephone	Open	Grid Ref	Acc	EM	PL	V	F	NS	D	S/B	E	Camp	S	T	DF
Mrs J Strudwick School House Bosherston Pembroke SA71 5DN	01646 661269	I to XII	SR 966947	Pr H	-	✓	-	✓	-	-	✓	-				
Mrs Linda Lawrence Keighley House Bosherston Pembroke SA71 5DP	01646 661436	IV to X	SR 966946	Pr H	-	-	✓	✓	-	✓	-	-				
Mr H Davies Warren Farm Warren Pembroke SA71 5HS	01646 661250	I to XII	SR 932975	Camp	-	-	-	-	-	-	-	-	basic	-	-	-
Mrs S Alderman Court Farm Castlemartin Pembroke SA71 5HE	01646 661228	I to XII	SR 916984	Farm	✓	✓	✓	✓	✓	✓	✓	-				
Mrs D Leese Ash Hay Castlemartin Pembroke SA71 5HN	01646 661345	V to IX	SR 913984	Pr H	-	✓	✓	✓	✓	✓	✓	-				
Mrs A Alderman West Farm The Old Vicarage Castlemartin Pembroke SA71 5HW	01646 661227	IV to IX	SR 908988	Farm & Camp	-	✓	✓	✓	✓	✓	✓	-	basic	✓	✓	-
Mrs R Smith Chapel Farm Castlemartin Pembroke SA71 5HW	01646 661312	I to XII	SR 907986	Farm	✓	✓	-	✓	✓	✓	-	-				
Mrs J A Watkins Gupton Farm Castlemartin Pembroke SA71 5HW	01646 661268	I to XII	SR 894989	Farm	✓	✓	-	✓	✓	✓	✓	-				
Mr G B Rees & Sons Castle Farm Angle SA71 5AR	01646 641220	IV to X	SM 865030	Camp	-	-	-	-	-	-	-	-	basic	✓	✓	-

Name and Address	Telephone	Open	Grid Ref	Acc	EM	PL	V	F	NS	D	S/B	E	Camp	S	T	DF
Mrs S Reece Timothy Lodge 39 Angle Village Pembroke SA71 5AT	01646 641342	IV to IX	SM 863029	Pr H	-	✓	✓	✓	✓	✓	✓	-				
Mrs N Pearce Merton Place House 3 East Back Pembroke SA71 4HL	01646 684796	I to XII	SM 987013	Pr H	-	-	-	✓	-	-	✓	-				
Mr & Mrs D Lightley Eaton Guest House 108 Main Street Pembroke SA71 4HN	01646 682517	I to XII	SM 988014	G H	✓	✓	✓	✓	✓	✓	✓	-				
Mrs Carole Hook 11 Springfield Terrace The Green Pembroke SA71 4NU	01646 685232	V to IX	SM 983017	G H	-	✓	✓	✓	✓	-	✓	-				
Mrs J Etherington Roxana Guest House Victoria Road Pembroke Dock SA72 6XU	01646 683116	I to XII	SM 963034	G H	✓	✓	✓	✓	✓	-	✓	✓				
Mr & Mrs G F Aylward The Welshman's Arms London Road Llanion Pembroke Dock SA72 6DS	01646 685643	I to XII	SM 971036	Inn	✓	✓	✓	✓	-	✓	✓	✓				
Mr & Mrs D Hawley Y Ffynnon 45 Honeyborough Road Great Honeyborough Neyland SA73 1RF	01646 601369	I to XII	SM 959062	Pr H	-	✓	-	✓	-	✓	✓	-				
Mr & Mrs H Fane The Lawrenny Castle Hotel High Street Neyland SA73 1SR	01646 601694	I to XII	SM 965051	Hotel	✓	✓	✓	✓	-	✓	✓	-				
Mr & Mrs B Fieldhouse Church Lakes Guest House 88 Church Road Llanstadwell Neyland SA73 1EA	01646 600840	I to XII	SM 965050	G H	✓	✓	✓	✓	-	✓	✓	-				

Name and Address	Telephone	Open	Grid Ref	Acc	EM	PL	V	F	NS	D	S/B	E	Camp	S	T	DF
Mr & Mrs S B Phillips Ferry Inn Hazelbeach Llanstadwell Neyland SA73 1EG	01646 600270	I to XII	SM 947048	Inn	✓	✓	✓	✓	-	-	✓	✓				
Mrs F M Simpson Pebbles Guest House 18-15 Pill Fold Milford Haven SA73 2NN	01646 698155	I to XII	SM 912059	G H	-	-	-	✓	-	-	✓	-				
Mrs M Binnion Cleddau Villa 21 St Anne's Road Hakin Milford Haven SA73 3LQ	01646 690313	I to XII	SM 899055	Pr H	-	✓		✓	-	-	✓	-				
Mrs P Morgan Ribbledene Gelliswick Road Hubberston Milford Haven SA73 3RG	01646 698966	III to X	SM 890063	Pr H	✓	✓	✓	✓	-	-	✓	-				
Mrs M Williams Skerry Back Farm Sandy Haven St Ishmael's Haverfordwest SA62 3DN	01646 636598	I to XII	SM 852073	Farm	✓	✓	✓	✓	✓	-	✓	-				
Georgina Llewellin Bicton St Ishmael's Haverfordwest SA62 3DR	01646 636215	III to X	SM 843078	Farm	✓	✓	✓	✓	-	✓	✓	✓				
Mr & Mrs J Llewellin Trewarren Farm St Ishmael's Haverfordwest SA62 3TJ	01646 636260	I to XII	SM 829071	Camp	-	-	-	-	-	-	-	-	basic	-	✓	✓
Mrs L Watts White Holmes Farm St Ishmael's Dale Haverfordwest SA62	01646 636251	I to XII	SM 817077	Farm & Camp	✓	✓	✓	✓	-	-	✓	-	basic	-	✓	-
Mrs G Davies Mullock Farm St Ishmael's Dale Haverfordwest SA62 3QS	01646 636230	I to XII	SM 818085	Farm & Camp	✓	✓	-	✓	-	-	✓	-	basic	-		-

Name and Address	Telephone	Open	Grid Ref	Acc	EM	PL	V	F	NS	D	S/B	E	Camp	S	T	DF
Mrs P Tamsett Eaton Hall Dale Haverfordwest SA62 3RB	01646 636293	IV to X	SM 811058	Pr H	-	✓	-	✓	-	-	✓	-				
Marloes Sands Y H Runwayskil. Marloes Haverfordwest SA62 3BH	01646 636667	III to X	SM 778080	Y H	-	-	-	✓	-	-	✓	-				
Mrs E Roddam-King Foxdale Glebe Lane Marloes Dale SA62 3AX	01646 636243	IV to X	SM 796083	G H & Camp	-	✓	✓	✓	-	✓	✓	✓	hol	✓	✓	✓
Mrs A Howe Greenacre Marloes Dale Haverfordwest SA62 3BE	01646 636400	I to XII	SM 792085	G H & Camp	✓	✓	✓	✓	-	✓	-	-	basic	✓	✓	-
Mrs B Price Fopston Farm St Bride's Dale SA62 3AW	01646 636271	I to XII	SM 798093	Farm	✓	✓	✓	✓	✓	✓	✓	-				
Mrs Hopkins Lower Broadmoor Farm Talbenny Little Haven SA62 3XD	01437 781219	I to XII	SM 820120	Farm & Camp	-	✓	-	✓	✓	-	✓	-	basic	-	✓	✓
Miss M Davies Howelston Farm Howelston Little Haven Broad Haven SA62 3UU	01437 781253	IV to IX	SM 851120	Camp	-	-	-	-	-	✓	-	-	hol	✓	✓	-
Mrs J Phillips Mount Pleasant 6 Settlands Hill Little Haven Broad Haven SA62 3LA	01437 781439	IV to X	SM 858129	Pr H	✓	✓	✓	✓	✓	✓	-	-				
Doreen Liddell St Brides Inn Little Haven Haverfordwest SA62 3UN	01437 781266	I to XII	SM 856128	Inn	✓	✓	✓	-	✓	✓	✓					

Name and Address	Telephone	Open	Grid Ref	Acc	EM	PL	V	F	NS	D	S/B	E	Camp	S	T	DF
Mrs C Porter Burton House Little Haven Broad Haven SA62 3UF	01437 781426	I to XII	SM 857128	G H	-	-	✓	✓	-	-	✓	-				
Mr & Mrs R Llewellin Whitegates Settlands Hill Little Haven Broad Haven SA62 3LA	01437 781552	I to XII	SM 857130	Pr H	✓	✓	✓	✓	-	✓	✓					
Broad Haven Y H Broad Haven Haverfordwest SA62 3JH	01437 781688	III to X	SM 863141	Y H	✓	✓	✓	✓	-	✓	-					
Mr A Mock Broad Haven Holiday Park Broad Haven SA62 3JD	01437 781277	V to IX	SM 864141	Camp	-	-	-	-	-	-	-		hol	✓	✓	✓
Mrs G Hopkins Glenfield 5 Atlantic Drive Broad Haven Haverfordwest SA62 3JA	01437 781502	I to XII	SM 864140	G H	-	✓	✓	✓	-	✓	-					
Mrs Morgan Ringstone Guest House Haroldston Hill Broad Haven SA62 3JP	01437 781051	I to XI	SM 862143	G H	-	✓	✓	-	-	✓	✓					
Mrs J Canton Nolton Haven Farm Nolton Haven Camrose SA62 11NH	01437 710263	I to XII	SM 859187	Farm	✓	✓	✓	✓	-	✓	✓					
Mr B Warner Wood Farm Newgale Haverfordwest SA62 6AR	01437 710253	III to X	SM 855218	Camp	-	-	-	-	-	-	-		hol	✓	✓	-
Mrs S Dixon Llys Aber 27 Main Street Solva Haverfordwest SA62 6UU	01437 721657	I to XII	SM 806243	Pr H	-	✓	✓	✓	-	✓	-					

Name and Address	Telephone	Open	Grid Ref	Acc	EM	PL	V	F	NS	D	S/B	E	Camp	S	T	DF
Mrs J Lawton The Old Pharmacy Restaurant Solva Haverfordwest		III to X	SM 806244	Pr H	✓	-	✓	✓	-	✓	✓	✓				
Eve Sendall The Smithy Solva Haverfordwest SA62 6UY	01437 721337	I to XII	SM 806244	Pr H	-	-	✓	✓	✓	-	✓	-				
Mrs M Bland Gamlyn 17 Yr Gribin Solva Haverfordwest SA62 6UY	01437 721542	III to X	SM 806243	Pr H	-	✓	✓	✓	-	-	✓	-				
Mrs J Hann Min Yr Afon 11 Yr Gribin Solva Haverfordwest SA62 6UY	01437 721752	I to XII	SM 806243	Pr H	-	✓	✓	✓	-	-	✓	-				
Michele Williams River View Cottage River Street Solva Haverfordwest SA62 6UX	01437 721679	I to XII	SM 806243	Pr H	-	✓	✓	✓	-	-	✓	✓				
Mr W Evans Caerfai Farm Caerfai St David's SA62 6QT	01437 720548	V to IX	SM 758244	Camp	-	-	-	-	-	-	-	-	hol	✓	✓	✓
Mrs E Davies Treginnis Uchaf St David's SA62 6RS	01437 720234	I to XII	SM 729244	Farm & Camp	-	✓	✓	✓	-	-	✓	✓	basic	-	-	-
Mr R Bateman Treginnis Lodge Lower Moor St David's SA62 6RS	01437 720524	I to XII	SM 734239	Camp	-	-	✓	✓	-	-	-	-	hol	-	✓	-
St David's Y H Llaethdy St David's Haverfordwest SA62 6PR	01437 720345	III to X	SM 739276	Y H	✓	✓	✓	✓	-	-	✓	-				

181

Name and Address	Telephone	Open	Grid Ref	Acc	EM	PL	V	F	NS	D	S/B	E	Camp	S	T	DF
Judy Griffiths Pwll-Caerog Farm Berea St David's SA62 6DG	01348 831682	VII to VIII	SM 786301	Farm & Camp	-	-	✓	✓	-	✓	✓	-	hol	-	✓	-
Mrs Evans Cwmwdig Water Guesthouse Berea Nr. St David's SA62 6DW	01348 831434	I to XII	SM 805304	G H	✓	✓	✓	✓	✓	✓	✓	✓				
Mr & Mrs Bull Ynys Barry Country Hotel Porth-gain St David's SA62 5BH	01348 831180	I to XII	SM 811319	G H	✓	✓	✓	✓	-	-	✓	✓				
Mrs M Bamsey Glan Y Mor Trefin Haverfordwest SA62 5AX	01348 837843	III to X	SM 839325	G H	✓	✓	✓	✓	-	✓	✓	-				
Trefin Youth Hostel 11 Ffordd-Yr-Afon Trefin Haverfordwest SA62 5AU	01348 831414	III to X	SM 840324	Y H	-	-	✓	-	-	-	✓	-				
Mr & Mrs S Pinner Maes-Y-Graig 18 Ffordd-Y-Felin Trefin Haverfordwest SA62 5AX	01348 831359	II to X	SM 839325	Pr H	-	✓	✓	✓	-	✓	-	-				
Mr & Mrs R Gratton Bryngarw Abercastle Road Trefin SA62 5AR	01348 831211	IV to X	SM 844327	G H	✓	✓	✓	✓	-	✓	✓	✓				
Pwll Deri Y H Castell Mawr Tref Asser Goodwick SA64 0LR	01348 5233	III to X	SM 891387	Y H	✓	✓	✓	✓	-	-	-	-	basic	✓	✓	-
Mr & Mrs R Lewis Fferm Tresinwen Strumble Head Goodwick SA64 0JL	01348 5621	I to XII	SM 901395	Camp	-	-	-	-	-	-	-	-	basic	-	✓	-

182

Name and Address	Telephone	Open	Grid Ref	Acc	EM	PL	V	F	NS	D	S/B	E	Camp	S	T	DF
Mrs E Trueman Villa Calabria New Hill Goodwick SA64 0DU	01348 874175	I to XII	SM 947388	Pr H	-	-	✓	✓	✓	-	✓	-				
Mrs T Colella Piccola Calabria New Hill Goodwick SA64 0DT	01348 873101	I to XII	SM 947388	Pr H			✓	✓	-	-	✓	-				
Monica Hendrie Stanley House Quay Road Goodwick SA64 0BS	01348 873024	I to XII	SM 946383	G H			✓	✓	✓	✓	✓	-				
Mr & Mrs Maxwell-Jones Coach House Cottage Glendower Square Goodwick Fishguard SA64 0DH	01348 873660	I to XII	SM 945383	Pr H	✓		✓	✓	✓	✓	✓	-				
Mr C Harries Fishguard Bay Caravan & Camping Site Dinas Cross Newport SA42 0YD	01348 6415	III to I	SM 983383	Camp	-	-	-	-	-	-	-	-	hol	✓	✓	✓
Mr & Mrs L Forrest Aux Pavots Pwllgwaelod Dinas Cross SA42 0SE	01348 6491	I to XII	SN 005399	Pr H	✓	-	-	✓	-	-	-	✓				
Mr H Harries Tycanol Farm Newport SA42 0ST	01239 820264	I to XII	SN 043395	Bunk & Camp	-	✓	-	✓	✓	✓	✓	-	basic	✓	✓	✓
Mr & Mrs B Watts Morawelon Camping Park Parrog Newport SA42 0RW	01239 820565	IV to X	SN 050397	Camp	-	-	-	-	-	-	-	-	hol	✓	✓	✓
Mr & Mrs D Inman 2 Spring Hill Parrog Road Newport SA42 0RH	01239 820626	I to XII	SN 054394	G H	✓	✓	✓	✓	✓	-	✓	-				

Name and Address	Telephone	Open	Grid Ref	Acc	EM	PL	V	F	NS	D	S/B	E	Camp	S	T	DF
Mr & Mrs C Joseph Hafan Deg Off Long Street Newport SA42 0TN	01239 820301	I to XII	SN 057393	Pr H	-	✓	✓	✓	-	✓	✓	-				
Ian & Penny Ross Llysmeddyg East Street Newport SA42 0SY	01239 820008	I to XII	SN 059392	G H	✓	✓	✓	✓	✓	-	✓	-				
Mrs A King Grove Park Guest House Pen-Y-Bont Newport SA42 0LT	01239 820122	I to XII	SN 061393	G H	✓	✓	✓	✓	-	✓	✓	✓				
Mrs B P Barnaby Fferm Y Cadno Moylegrove Cardigan SA43 3BT	01239 86684	IV to IX	SN 102443	Farm	-	✓	✓	✓	-	✓	✓	-				
Mr & Mrs D Jenkins Cwm Connell Coastal Cottages Cwm Connell Moylgrove Nr Cardigan SA43 3BX	01239 86691	III to I	SN 119461	Farm	✓	✓	✓	✓	-	✓	✓	✓				
Mr H Biddyr Allt-Y-Goed Poppit Sands St Dogmael's Cardigan SA43 3LPP	01239 612673	I to XII	SN 135494	Camp	-	-	-	-	-	-	-	-	hol	✓	✓	✓
Poppit Sands Y H Sea View Poppit Cardigan SA43 3LP	01239 612936	II to XI	SN 144487	Y H	-	-	✓	✓	-	-	✓	-	basic	✓	✓	-
Mrs S Sharp Glan-Y-Mor Poppit Sands St Dogmael's Cardigan SA43 3PL	01239 612329	I to XII	SN 147487	Pr H	-	✓	✓	✓	✓	✓	✓	-				

Name and Address	Telephone	Open	Grid Ref	Acc	EM	PL	V	F	NS	D	S/B	E	Camp	S	T	DF
Mrs J Thomas Briar Bank Poppit Sands St Dogmael's Cardigan SA43 3LR	01239 612339	III to X	SN 163468	Pr H	✓	✓	✓	✓	✓	✓	✓	-				
Mrs R Antwis Nant-Y-Pele Feidr Fawr St Dogmael's Cardigan SA43 3EU	01239 613590	IV to X	SN 162462	Pr H	✓	-	✓	✓	-	-	✓	-				
J Beckingham Argo Villa Poppit Sands St Dogmael's Cardigan SA43 3LF	01239 613031	I to XII	SN 162462	Pr H	-	-	-	✓	-	-	✓	-				

DISTANCE CHART

The table summarises the places where accommodation is listed in the guide and shows the distance between each. The availability of public transport is also indicated to help those planning day walks

Place	Accomm choices	Dist from previous stage (km)	Dist from previous stage(Mls)	Served by transport
Amroth	2	-	-	yes
Wiseman's Bridge	2	3.4	2.1	yes
Saundersfoot	5	1.9	1.2	yes
Tenby	6	6.1	3.8	yes
Penally (Valleyfield Top)	3	5.0	3.1	yes
Lydstep	1	1.9	1.2	yes
Manorbier	2 + YH	6.3	3.9	yes
Freshwater East	2	5.5	3.4	yes
Broad Haven	3	8.8	5.5	yes
Castlemartin	6	12.9	8.0	yes
Angle	2	16.6	10.3	yes
Pembroke	3	18.3	11.4	yes
Pembroke Dock	2	5.6	3.5	yes
Neyland	4	5.8	3.6	yes
Milford Haven	3	9.0	5.6	yes
Sandy Haven	4	7.2	4.5	close
Dale	2	9.2	5.7	yes
West Dale	as above	9.8	6.1	yes
Marloes Sands	YH	3.4	2.1	close
Musselwick	2	7.6	4.7	yes
St Bride's	1	3.5	2.2	-
Little Haven	6	9.0	5.6	yes
Broad Haven	3 + YH	1.0	0.6	yes
Nolton Haven	1	5.6	3.5	-
Newgale	1	3.5	2.2	yes
Solfach (Solva)	7	8.7	5.4	yes
Caerfai	1	6.9	4.3	yes
St Non's	2	1.1	0.7	yes

Place	Accomm choices	Dist from previous stage (km)	Dist from previous stage(Mls)	Served by transport
Porth Mawr	YH	12.7	7.9	-
Abereiddi	2	12.2	7.6	close
Porth-gain	1	3.2	2.0	close
Trefin	3 + YH	2.7	1.7	yes
Pwll Deri	YH	15.6	9.7	-
Strumble Head	1	4.5	2.8	-
Wdig (Goodwick)	4	10.3	6.4	yes
Cwm-yr-Eglwys	2	15.1	9.4	close
Newport	6 + YH	5.3	3.3	yes
Ceibwr	2	14.5	9.0	-
St Dogmael's	5	11.4	7.1	yes

ACCESS POINTS

The table gives the grid references for the main points at which there is access from the Coast Path to the road. There is not necessarily formal car parking at these places, therefore, if leaving a car, please remember to park considerately, paying particular attention not to block field accesses or create obstructions for other road users.

Amroth	(SN 161 070)
Wiseman's Bridge	(SN 145 061)
Coppet Hall	(SN 139 054)
Rhode Wood	(SN 138 042)
Monkstone Point	(SN 144 032)
Waterwynch Bay	(SN 134 021)
Tenby (North)	(SN 133 014)
Tenby (South)	(SN 129 001)
Penally	(SS 123 989)
Valleyfield Top	(SS 109 984)
Lydstep Point	(SS 087 978)
Skrinkle Haven	(SS 077 973)
Manorbier Bay	(SS 061 975)
Swanlake Bay	(SS 045 980)
Freshwater East	(SS 015 977)
Stackpole Quay	(SR 992 957)
Broad Haven	(SR 977 938)
St Govan's Chapel	(SR 966 930)
Elegug Stacks	(SR 926 946)
Freshwater West	(SR 885 997)
West Angle	(SM 853 031)
Angle village	(SM 866 029)
Rhoscrowther	(SM 897 021)
Pwllcrochan	(SM 921 029)
Pembroke Power Station	(SM 925 023)
Goldborough Pill	(SM 944 010)
Hundleton	(SM 955 007)
Quoit's Mill	(SM 967 011)
Pembroke	(SM 982 018)
Pembroke Dock (South)	(SM 965 026)
Hazel Beach	(SM 946 047)

Milford Haven (East)	(SM 923 059)
Gelliswick	(SM 885 056)
Sandy Haven	(SM 856 075)
Longberry Point	(SM 840 067)
Monk Haven	(SM 828 064)
Musselwick Point	(SM 820 065)
The Gann	(SM 814 069)
Pickleridge	(SM 808 066)
Dale Fort	(SM 821 052)
St Ann's Head	(SM 805 031)
Westdale Bay	(SM 790 059)
Marloes Sands	(SM 787 072)
Marloes Sands	(SM 781 076)
Watery Bay	(SM 769 079)
Martin's Haven	(SM 760 089)
Musselwick Sands	(SM 785 089)
St Bride's	(SM 802 109)
Mill Haven	(SM 816 123)
Goultrop Roads	(SM 846 122)
Musselwick Bay	(SM 850 123)
Little Haven	(SM 855 129)
Broad Haven	(SM 861 141)
Haroldston Chins	(SM 863 163)
Druidston Haven	(SM 862 172)
Nolton Haven	(SM 859 186)
Newgale	(SM 849 219)
Newgale	(SM 847 224)
Pointz Castle	(SM 827 231)
St Elvis	(SM 812 236)
Solfach (Solva)	(SM 806 243)
Nine Wells	(SM 786 243)
Caer Bwdy	(SM 766 244)
Caerfai Bay	(SM 759 243)
St Non's	(SM 752 242)
Porth Clais	(SM 741 242)
Porthstinian	(SM 724 252)
Porth Mawr	(SM 733 271)
Penberry	(SM 764 292)

Abereiddi	(SM 797 312)
Traeth Llyfn	(SM 803 319)
Porth-gain	(SM 815 324)
Aber Draw	(SM 834 324)
Aber Castle	(SM 853 336)
Pwllstrodur	(SM 866 337)
Aber Mawr	(SM 882 345)
Aber-bach	(SM 884 350)
Pwll Crochan	(SM 886 363)
Pwll Deri	(SM 894 384)
Strumble Head	(SM 897 413)
Porthsychan	(SM 905 407)
Penrhyn	(SM 912 407)
Cwm Felin	(SM 925 400)
Wdig (Goodwick)	(SM 949 392)
Abergwaun (Fishguard)	(SM 962 375)
Penrhyn	(SM 983 383)
Hes'cwm	(SM 997 386)
Pwllgwaelod	(SN 004 399)
Cwm-yr-Eglwys	(SN 015 400)
Cwm-yr-Eglwys	(SN 017 398)
Aber Fforest	(SN 025 395)
Aber Rhigian	(SN 032 395)
Parrog	(SN 051 396)
Nyfer Bridge	(SN 062 394)
Newport Sands	(SN 054 405)
Traeth Bach	(SN 101 450)
Ceibwr Bay	(SN 110 457)
Pwllygranant	(SN 122 478)
Allt-y-Goed	(SN 135 494)

191

Printed by CARNMOR PRINT & DESIGN
95-97 LONDON ROAD, PRESTON, LANCASHIRE, UK.